THE CSQ3® SOLUTION

Cost, **S**chedule, and **Q**uality
raised to the **3**rd Power

Achieve
Organizational Excellence!

CSQ3 Corporation

www.csq3.com

Illustrations and Cover Design by John Ullrick

Library of Congress Control Number: 2010913213

First Printing

ISBN 978-0-9815877-0-7

ISBN 978-0-9815877-1-4 (eBook)

ISBN 978-0-9815877-2-1 (audio book)

Jon,

THANK YOU FOR YOUR FRIENDSHIP!

Frank Kozwara

Dedication

The CSQ3® Solution is dedicated to my wife, my family, and to the employees, volunteers, and managers that strive to achieve "Organizational Excellence."

Contents

The CSQ3® Solution is a journey that will positively change the culture of organizations. Personnel will become empowered. Departments will become Centers of Knowledge. Managers will guide the organization to Excellence. True Performance will be Recognized and Rewarded.

Frank Koczwara

CSQ3® Solution Overview

The easiest way to explain the development of the CSQ3® Solution would be to go through the experiences and worldwide adventures as they relate to the evolution of the methodologies but, that would take too long. However, readers need to know that there is a method to the madness. Hence, I have included key development and overview material in this opening section.

Note: the other sections of the book are more fun. Generally, reading about organizational performance improvement is just about as much fun as watching paint dry. Consequently, I made it an adventure. Set in a Renaissance time frame, the Loyal Subject is challenged to improve the performance of the Land of Near. The Land of Near represents a typical organization, where upper management sets the direction and the various departments fight for power. Loyal Subject's challenges explain the CSQ3® Solution. So if you need additional background information, continue reading. If you want to start the adventure, go to the next chapter, "Loyal Subject – Taking Up the Call to Duty."

Leading a Worldwide Benchmarking Effort

It was a no-brainer for management to authorize a worldwide benchmarking effort once they saw the Business Roundtable[1] statistics. (The Business Roundtable is an association of chief executive officers of leading U.S. companies.) Best in class organizations are achieving Cost, Schedule, and Quality excellence in the work they perform! Cost, Schedule, and Quality; all at the same time!! Performance gains are substantial!!!

The worldwide benchmarking effort that I led was intense, fact filled, and yielded extremely useful information and observations. Besides the thousands of pages of material and reports, in reflection, I was left with the following common sense observations: One: "Clearly establish what you are going to do, before doing it" and two: "Departments build walls." Multi-department work efforts get thrown over the walls from one department to the next creating significant inefficiencies in the overall performance of an organization.

Based on the benchmarking results, management approved a major improvement effort. The effort was focus on improving just one department. It ended up changing the entire organization.

Directing Major Improvement Effort

Directing a major improvement effort was tough. We didn't have a pathway to move forward. We didn't have a framework to use. We were starting from scratch. New ground and new ideas were being explored.

The organization wanted the performance improvement answer. The Business Roundtable and benchmarking results substantiated the prize. We formulated our material, and presented it to the organization. Organizational acceptance was exceptional. It was a start. Further substantiation and validation in the real world was needed.

Consulting Worldwide

The major improvement effort then led to worldwide implementation and consulting assignments. The learning experiences were exciting and fun. Work effort teams were inspired. The interaction and communication between management and work effort teams was excellent. You could feel the cultural change in the organization. Gone were the days of dictators. Gone were the days of doing what's best for the department. The focus was on obtaining the best organizational solution for any given opportunity. Management direction and decisions were sought after and respected. My consulting assignments included projects, major commercial deals, strategic efforts, operational efforts, and special management initiatives throughout the world.

Breakthrough: New Country Entry

In fact, one of the most fruitful consulting assignments was "New Country Entry." The executives in the organization were always getting requests to enter new areas or join forces in new ventures but, they did not have an effective system for handling the work. The work was assigned to an individual or a team, and they would eventually deliver an answer. Executives were not satisfied with the consistency and quality of the process. Hence, the purpose of the "New Country Entry" consulting assignment was to significantly improve the work flow process. Well, it doesn't get any bigger than this. Imagine deciding if your organization should enter a major new area of the world! With 50 of the brightest people in the organization, we tackled the problem. Guess what? The same work flow system that I applied to major commercial deals and projects was also applicable to strategic work efforts. The CSQ3® Solution was born...

Achieving Cost, Schedule, and Quality Excellence

Achieving Cost, Schedule, and Quality excellence in every work effort in the organization is the heart of the CSQ3® Solution. Achieving Cost and Schedule excellence is easy to understand (provide the lowest cost and fastest schedule) but, what is Quality? Isn't it a nebulous term? Well, in the common sense land of CSQ3®, Quality is the "Delivery of Value" and the "Making of Sound Decisions."

Results: Savings of $240 million a year

For information, how did that original improvement effort turn out? Savings in Cost alone were estimated at $20,000,000 per month[2] or about $240 million in a work effort system of about $1.2 billion per year. In fact, management stated[3] that "The improvement effort had the highest Return on Investment (ROI) in the history of a major international oil company."

With respect to the savings:

- What is the non-compounded 5 year result?
    - $240 million x 5 years = $1.2 billion (The calculation does not include additional savings due to Schedule and Quality enhancements).
- Why is the Return On Investment (ROI) so high?
    - The potential return is so high because the capital cost of implementation is so low and productivity gains are so significant. You are investing in your own people. All personnel in the organization will utilize the same performance improvement methodology. (Most importantly, the CSQ3® Solution is industry independent. The Solution is applicable to profit, non-profit, or government organizations of any size).

What is the CSQ3® Solution?

So what is the CSQ3® Solution? The Solution is made up of three Powers: CSQ3® Fundamentals, Optimum, and Metrics. CSQ3® Fundamentals is a performance improvement methodology that is applicable to all personnel and all work efforts in the organization. CSQ3® Optimum is a multilevel organizational work flow system built on the principles taught in CSQ3® Fundamentals. CSQ3® Metrics is an organizational performance scoring system built on the utilization of CSQ3® Optimum. CSQ3® Metrics uses a point system to track and measure an organization's progress towards achieving excellence.

CSQ3® is Cost, Schedule, and Quality Raised to the 3rd Power.

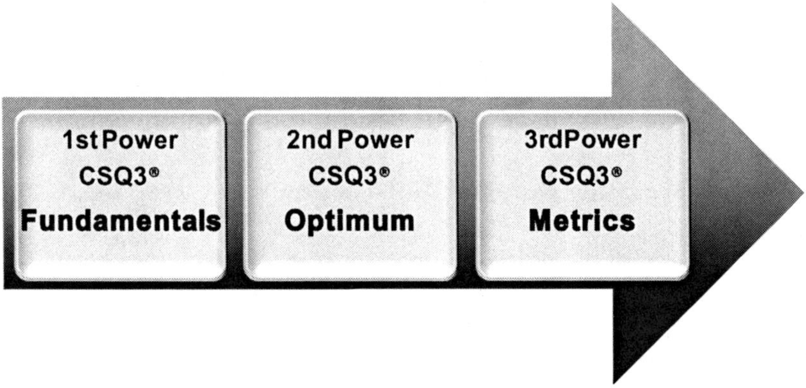

Figure 1

1st Power - CSQ3® Fundamentals

CSQ3® Fundamentals has the power to improve the performance of all work efforts in an organization. A work effort has a definable objective; a start and an end point; numerous tasks or activities; and measurable results or goals. A work effort may take minutes, hours, days, months, or even years.

Establish Clear Work Effort Scopes

Work efforts range in scope and perspective. From an individual perspective, typical work efforts might include: mowing the lawn, painting a room, buying a car, buying a house, or planning for retirement. From an organizational perspective, work efforts might include: filling orders, performing maintenance, building new facilities, signing new deals, considering new joint ventures, etc.

Establish a clear scope for any work effort by answering the questions. What are we going to do? Why are we doing it? What does success look like?

Utilize a Common Work Effort Structure

"Clearly identify what you are going to do before doing it." It sounds so simple; yet, it is so often not performed. Excuses abound. It takes too long. I already know the answer. We will do it on the fly, etc. Utilize a common work effort structure. CSQ3® methodology breaks work efforts into phases, with decision points between each phase. Each phase has a specific objective. Once the current phase objective is completed, decide if the work effort should progress to the next phase.

Report Cost, Schedule, and Quality Information

For every work effort report Cost, Schedule, and Quality information. Cost and Schedule information is easy to understand when one asks: "How much will it cost?" "How long will it take?"

The CSQ3® Solution defines Quality as the "Delivery of Value" and the "Making of Sound Decisions." Hence besides reporting Cost and Schedule estimates, Value estimates are developed. Report Value estimates in economic terms, such as Return on Investment. The easiest way to report decisions is with Decision Tables. Decision Tables include work effort decisions, risk mitigation decisions, options, and direction.

Teach the Entire Organization

Worldwide consulting validated by the "New Country Entry" work demonstrated the applicability of a common work flow process in an organization. Teach CSQ3® Fundamentals to the entire organization.

The following figure highlights the elements that will be discussed in CSQ3® Fundamentals:

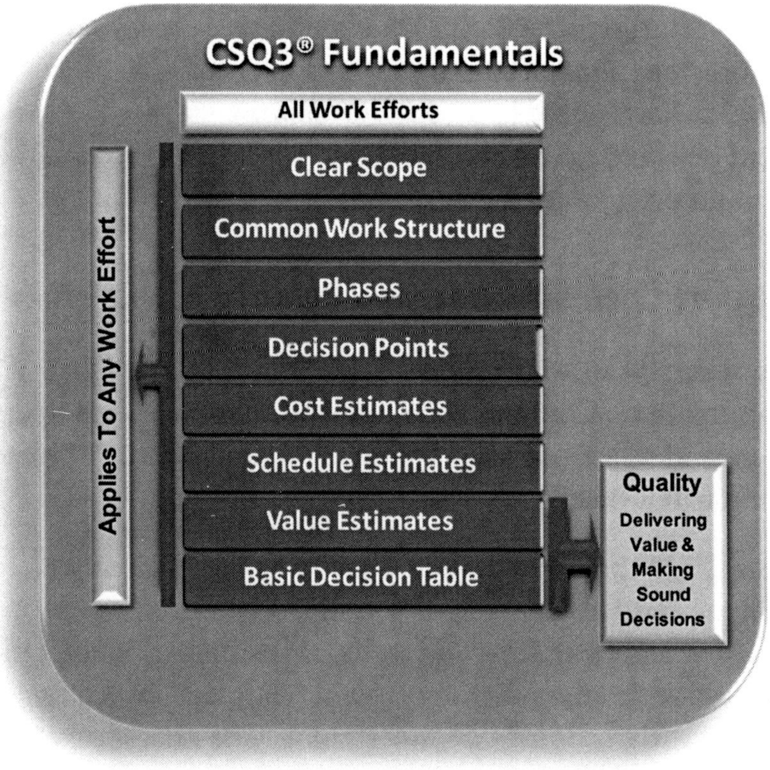

Figure 2

So what will happen if everyone in the organization speaks the same work flow language?

- One, individual and departmental work efforts will improve.
- Two, the organization will have a better understanding of the departmental work being performed.
- Three, personnel placed on teams to work on multi-department opportunities will understand how the work effort will move forward.

2nd Power - CSQ3® Optimum

CSQ3® Optimum is a multilevel organizational workflow system that has the power to eliminate the walls and kingdoms that departments build. CSQ3® Optimum assumes an understanding of the basic elements in CSQ3® Fundamentals.

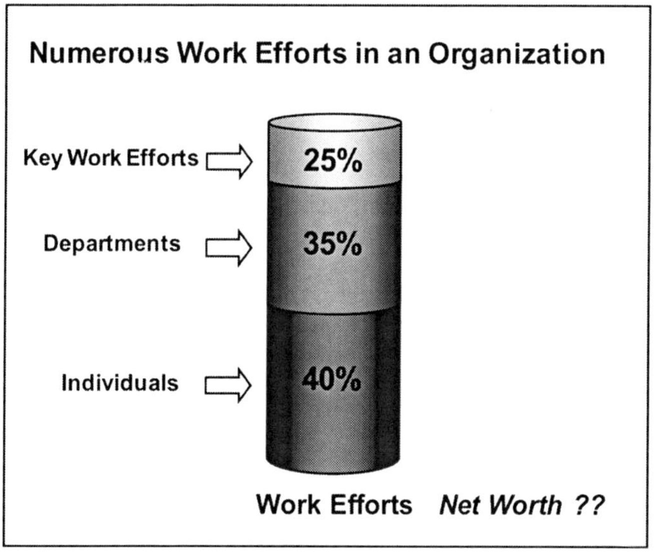

Figure 3

There are numerous work efforts in an organization. For simplicity, individual, department, and key organizational work efforts are shown in the Figure. The percentages shown in the Figure are representative, and will vary from organization to organization. CSQ3® Optimum focuses on key organizational work efforts.

A key organizational work effort is a work effort that requires multi-department input, or is a department work effort designated by management to be included in the CSQ3® Optimum workflow system. All key organizational work efforts are to be included in the CSQ3® Optimum workflow system.

An example of a department work effort that management might designated to be in the CSQ3® Optimum workflow system would be a secret research project. The research department may claim total ownership but, in reality if the work effort is successful, numerous organizational departments will need to be involved.

Typical CSQ3® Optimum work efforts might include: building a new facility; capturing a major commercial deal; or establishing a new strategic direction for the organization. In most cases, key organizational work efforts have a large net worth to the organization.

Remember Me

Key Work Efforts have a Large Net Worth to the Organization

CSQ3® Optimum is an overall organizational work flow system. Include all key strategic, major commercial and project work efforts in the system.

Additional Work Effort Requirements

There are additional requirements in CSQ3® Optimum that need highlighting. The additional requirements include:

- **Management Decision Points:** Decision Points between Phases become formal Management Decision Points. At a formal Management Decision Point, management has only two decision options: "Approve" the work effort; the work effort moves to the next phase. "Kill" the work effort; the work effort stops. Redoing a work effort phase is not permitted. The never ending work effort has just ended.

- **Advanced Decision Tables:** Decision tables are required. Include controllable decisions, risk mitigation decisions, the department accountable for each decision, and variations in risk profile paths.

- **Execution Plus®:** Utilize a standardized documentation procedure. Execution Plus®, which is a work effort documentation methodology simplifies and standardizes the reporting requirements of work effort teams.

Requires Organizational Governance

Management needs to establish, and govern the CSQ3® Optimum work flow system. The work flow system contains all key work efforts in the organization. Critical management governance items include the following:

- **Creation of Work Efforts:** Assuming that there are several competing ideas for a similar work effort, what work effort will be created and how will it be placed in the organization?

- **Establishment of Scope:** What is the scope for each created work effort?

- **Empowering Teams:** The CSQ3® Solution is focused on multi-department empowered teams. Management needs to provide a culture of true empowerment.

- **Assigning Resources**: Management needs to provide the necessary monetary and personnel resources to work efforts.

- **Tracking Responsibility and Risk**: Work effort teams will report department and risk related information. Tracking of the reported information is required.

- **Managing the Three Level System:** CSQ3® Optimum is a three level organizational work flow system. The three levels are Strategic, Major Commercial, and Project. Managing the system will require resources.

If Properly Implemented:

So what is the end result if an organization properly implements CSQ3® Optimum? Overtime, individuals in the organization will be saying: "The organization is Performing the Right Work, at the Right Time, with the Right People." The following highlights CSQ3® Optimum elements:

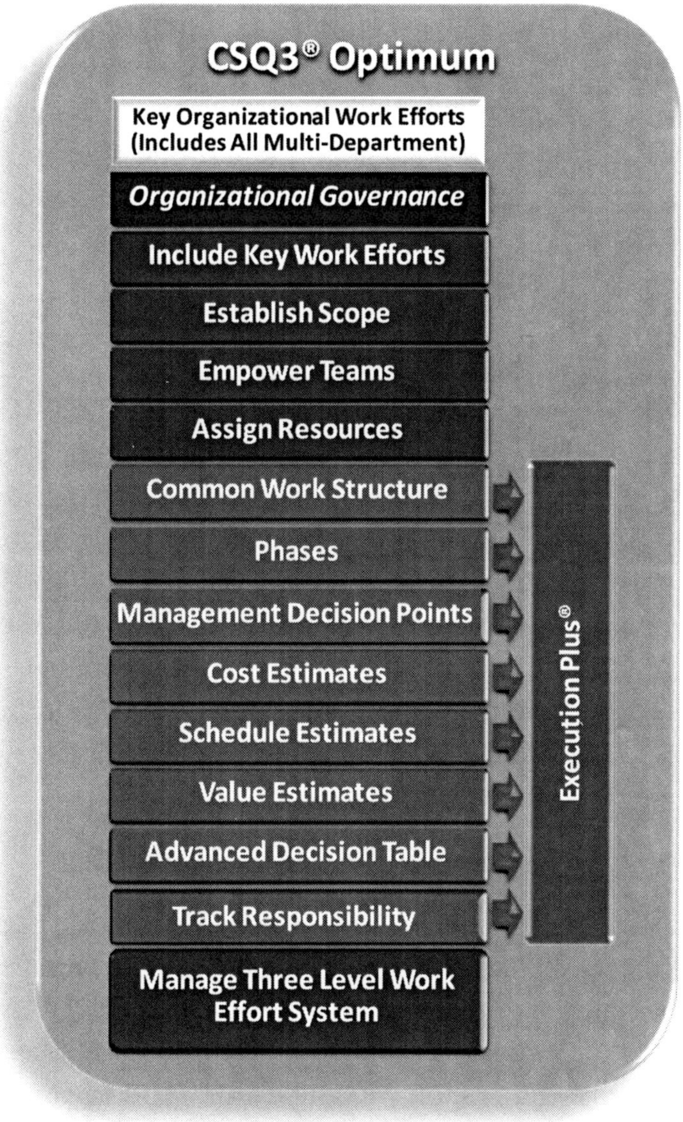

Figure 4

3rd Power - CSQ3® Metrics

CSQ3® Metrics is an organizational performance scoring system that has the power to focus the organization on the delivery of value and the creation of a self-correcting organization. The 10,000 point (maximum) organizational performance scoring system is based on the use of CSQ3® Optimum in an organization. The CSQ3® Metrics performance scoring system allocates a maximum of 6,000 points to the delivery of value and 4,000 points to the creation of a self correcting organization.

Delivering Value

CSQ3® Metrics includes the evaluation of all CSQ3® Optimum work efforts that have reached the final work effort phase. Estimated and actual work effort values are compared to obtain a score for each evaluated work effort. The maximum point award for any one work effort is 2,000 points. Evaluated work efforts are prorated at each CSQ3® Optimum level with the maximum score per level as follows: Strategic Level 2,000 Points, Major Commercial Level 2,000 Points, and Project Level 2,000 Points.

Creating a Self Correction Organization

Four thousand points are awarded to the creation of a self-correcting organization. The point awards are focused on the training, implementation, and use of CSQ3® methodology with special emphasis on improving work effort teams and organizational departments. The maximum point award breakdown is as follows: Training, Utilization, and Data Capturing 2,000 Points, Improving Work

Efforts 1,000 Points, and Improving Departments 1,000 Points.

The figure below highlights the elements that will be discussed in CSQ3® Metrics:

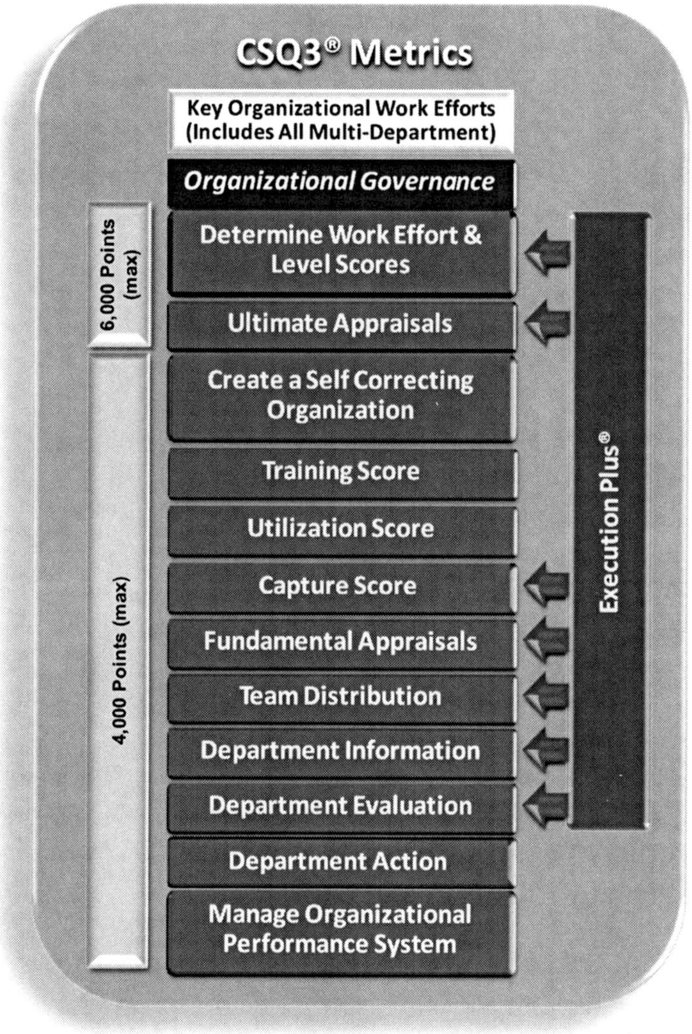

Figure 5

CSQ3® Metrics uses documented work effort information to establish awarded point scores. In addition, knowledge and insight established from Appraisals substantiates the recommendations and actions to improve the organization.

Organizational Excellence

In summary, the CSQ3® Solution is a simple; yet, sophisticated formula for improving the performance of any organization. The methodology and systems are built on sound principles, and the end result is an organization that strives to achieve Cost, Schedule, and Quality excellence.

Flow of the Book

Let's face it. Writing a book about improving performance and work flow in an organization would put anyone to sleep. So let's make it an adventure.

The adventure is set in the Renaissance Era, a time of change. The main character is "Loyal Subject." Loyal Subject is from the "Land of Near."

The "Supreme Ruler" rules over the entire Land of Near.

The Land of Near represents an organization. Supreme Ruler represents executive management and, Loyal Subject is challenged with improving performance.

Organizational performance is extremely poor. The People of Near are angry. The Supreme Ruler needs Loyal Subject's help. Loyal Subject needs to bring the Land of Near back to Greatness.

Supreme Ruler presents Loyal Subject with three challenges. If successful, Loyal Subject will be greatly rewarded.

The challenges highlight the Powers of the CSQ3® Solution. Fortunately, to aid in the quest, Loyal Subject has the ability to see into the future.

- Challenge #1 teach **CSQ3® Fundamentals**. CSQ3® Fundamentals gives everyone in the organization the power to speak the same work flow language.
- Challenge #2 teach **CSQ3® Optimum**, which is an organizational work flow system. CSQ3® Optimum eliminates department walls and gives an organization the power to perform the right work, at the right time, with the right people.
- Challenge #3 teach **CSQ3® Metrics**, which is an organizational performance scoring system. Note, organizations scoring 9,000 points or more in the 10,000 point system are classified as achieving "Organizational Excellence."

Achieve Organizational Excellence

The Loyal Subject has a special gift of future gaze: the ability to see the future. The people in the Land of Near are angry; they are no longer competitive in the changing world. The Supreme Ruler has heard from wizards about "The CSQ3® Solution." The Supreme Ruler asks "The Loyal Subject" to look into the future; learn the Powers of the CSQ3® Solution; and save the Land of Near.

Loyal Subject - Taking Up the Call to Duty

The Loyal Subject, who has the gift of future gaze, is from the village of Hope in the Land of Near. The Supreme Ruler of Near is troubled. Costs are too high; Schedules are too long; and, Quality is non-existent. Our people are losing their jobs. We are becoming non-competitive with distant lands. The nobles in the various provinces are more interested in their own power and wealth, than in the wealth and well being of the Land of Near. The work performed by the provinces from an overall perspective is mediocre at best. (Note: the Land of Near is a typical organization and the provinces are the departments in the organization.) Loyal Subject, I need your help!

Loyal, for short, heeds the call. What can I do? There are many people in our land and numerous provinces. I am just one person; but, with a gift to see the future.

From past experiences, the Supreme Ruler knows that all work efforts need clear scopes. With sincerity in his eyes Supreme Ruler says "I have faith in you. I give you three challenges. If you can successfully complete the challenges, you will receive numerous rewards, and the Land of Near will become Great Again!" Supreme Ruler (Executive Management) presents Loyal Subject (person responsible for CSQ3® implementation) with the 1st challenge....

Challenge #1 - The Power of CSQ3® Fundamentals "Everyone Speaks the Same Work Flow Language"

What do you want me to do? Teach work effort fundamentals to the populous.

Why do you want me to do it? So everyone in the land can understand that Cost, Schedule, and Quality excellence is achievable in every work effort.

What does success look like?

- All of the populous understands the fundamentals.
- Nobles (Department Management) understand their roles and responsibilities.
- The populous uses the fundamentals in their own work efforts.
- Work efforts are consistently implemented with Cost, Schedule, and Quality excellence.

Loyal Subject is puzzled. Achieving Cost, Schedule, and Quality excellence at the same time! There is quiet. Loyal goes into "future gaze." With the ability to see the future, Loyal sees the following:

Cost: "…best company is spending 72 cents of the industry average dollar for the same functional scope."

The information is from the Roundtable[1] so it must be true. The referenced best company is achieving Cost, Schedule, and Quality excellence in their work efforts.

Loyal Subject agrees to the 1st Challenge !

Supreme Ruler is pleased. The Ruler knows that the people of Near want change. Their livelihood depends on becoming the best. The people can relate to Loyal Subject's goal.

The next challenge is going to be more difficult. On key work efforts, work efforts that have a significant net worth to the people of Near, the Supreme Ruler uses the following provinces (departments):

Intellectus: For every key work effort the province of Intellectus determines what needs to be done.

Thunder: The province of Thunder implements key work efforts.

Pain: The province of Pain operates all key work efforts.

Supreme Ruler is furious with the Provinces of Intellectus, Thunder, and Pain. The provinces do not communicate with one another. The provinces fight for control, and are content to play political games. Key work efforts that are necessary for the growth of the Land of Near are suffering. Supreme Ruler presents Loyal Subject with the 2nd challenge….

Challenge #2 - The Power of CSQ3® Optimum "Perform the Right Work, at the Right Time, with the Right People"

What do you want me to do? Implement a work effort system that will contain all key organizational work efforts in the land, simplify their management, and improve their performance.

Why do you want me to do it? The antics of Intellectus, Thunder, and Pain are destroying the future of Near!

What does success look like?

- Agreement is obtained for the future strategic direction of Near. Additional strategic efforts are to be handled swiftly, yet with great thought.
- Major new contracts are signed with new opportunities for our people.
- The major contracts will lead to the building of new shops and the opening up of more opportunities, so that our people can go back to work and Near can grow.
- Key organizational work efforts can be managed and viewed from an overall perspective; yet, management will have the ability to zoom in and focus on the smaller components of each.

Loyal Subject's knees are weak. The Nobles of Intellectus, Thunder, and Pain are very formidable. However, the people in the provinces are dedicated to the Land of Near. If Loyal had more support information, perhaps activities could be refocused; but wait, Loyal saw the future on Cost. What does the Roundtable[1] say about Schedule? Going into future gaze, Loyal sees the following:

Schedule: "...fastest company takes only 70 percent as long as the industry average to bring a project from a business idea to a facility in production"

Whoa!! Cost at 72 cents on the dollar and Schedule at 70% as long. Achieving Cost, Schedule, and Quality excellence has some definite advantages.

Loyal Subject agrees to the 2nd Challenge !!

Supreme Ruler is glad. Now, for the greatest challenge of all: The Nobles in the Land of Near are very short term focused. Our people do not have enough food to eat; yet, they dine on the best game, pay themselves huge bonuses, and live the life of luxury. Their bonuses are based on next quarter's profit without looking further into the future. A machine that is not properly maintained (because production cannot stop since bonuses are tied to production) will produce today but, not in the future. The Provinces are not producing Value and the decisions that are being made are not of the highest quality.

Challenge #3 - The Power of CSQ3® Metrics "Achieve Organizational Excellence"

What do you want me to do? Implement a performance measuring system that is applicable across the land. Measure our success with key work efforts and with our ability to continually improve over time.

Why do you want me to do it? The performance systems of the past are unfair and inadequate. Extremely high rewards are paid for short term success; where the short term successes, in the longer term, are damaging the Land of Near.

What does success look like?

- For all key work efforts, measure estimated Value to Actual Delivered Value.
- Measure the understanding of Cost, Schedule, and Quality principles in the land.
- Provide honest feedback so that our people involved with key work efforts can improve.
- Provide honest feedback so that we can improve our provinces (departments).

Loyal Subject is bewildered. How can any performance measurement system do all of the Challenge items? However, Loyal is not deterred. Going into future gaze, Loyal once again consults the Roundtable[1] for understanding about the possibility of a land that achieves Cost, Schedule, and Quality excellence. It is extremely important:

Quality: "...best company transforms a 15 percent Return on Investment (ROI) project...into a 22.5 percent ROI project... In contrast poorest performers turn that same project into a 9 percent ROI."

Return on Investment (ROI) is a financial matter, a Value measurement. Loyal doesn't understand financial matters.

Loyal consults with a friend, "Good Friend." "Loyal, if you saved $1000 and put it in the bank at an interest rate of 2% per year; in five years, you would have $1,104. At 9% per year you would have $1,530, and at 22.5% per year you would have $2,758. At what ROI would you want to put your money?" Loyal's eyes light up. It is good to have a Good Friend.

Loyal Subject weighs the potential gain for completing the adventure; and, commits to the 3rd Challenge…

Let the Battles Begin !!!

The Supreme Ruler has given the Loyal Subject the challenge of teaching CSQ3® Fundamentals to the Populous. Loyal Subject's "future gaze" (the ability to see the future) sees the following:

Everyone in the Land of Near is speaking the same work flow language. The work efforts are different but, the understanding on how to effectively implement the work is clear!

Challenge # 1: Winning Over the Populous (Teaching CSQ3® Fundamentals)

Loyal Subject needs to understand CSQ3® Fundamentals before being able to teach the fundamentals to the people of Near. Loyal mind melds with a writer in the future.

Improving an organization takes time. However, if the fundamentals are valid and understandable, the time it takes to see real results can be significantly shorted. Organizations perform work. The work efforts vary in scope. Some scopes can be accomplished on an individual basis. Some scopes involve the creation of work effort teams with team members being pulled together to solve group, department, or overall organizational objectives or opportunities. In all cases, the same CSQ3® work flow methodology applies.

That means personnel dealing with strategic matters, going after major commercial deals, building new facilities, running a department, or in operations, can utilize the same fundamental work flow methodology. Obviously, the focus of the work efforts will be different, and the talents of the personnel working on the various work efforts will not be the same but, there will be a common understanding of what each work effort is trying to accomplish as the work effort travels to completion.

Before Launching a Work Effort, Provide a Clear Scope

Every work effort needs a clear scope. Establish a clear work effort scope by answering the questions: What is the work effort going to do? Why are we doing it? What does success look like? As an example, the Supreme Ruler clearly established Loyal Subject's work effort challenges.

However, before going any further, let's talk more about work efforts.

Work Efforts

First of all what is a work effort? In general, a work effort has a definable objective; a start and an end point; numerous tasks or activities; and measurable results or goals.

Work Effort

- **Definable objective**
- **Start and end points**
- **Numerous tasks or activities**
- **Measurable results or goals**

Hence, planning and implementing a retirement plan is a work effort. Building a house is a work effort. Designing and constructing a new manufacturing facility is a work effort.

Work Effort Examples

- Individual
  - Plant a garden
- Functional Group (more than one individual)
  - Develop a specification
- Department (numerous groups)
  - Implement a Maintenance Program
- Organization (numerous departments)
  - Build a manufacturing plant
  - Negotiate a major deal
  - Take over another organization

A work effort is a project. However, a CSQ3® work effort is more than just building things. Let's consider securing a major commercial deal. There are numerous internal and external factors to consider. Numerous organizational entities may need to be consulted or may be affected by the commercial deal (finance, legal, operations, etc.). There is no guarantee that the commercial deal will be signed. However, a well thought out and carefully established plan for capturing the deal (clearly identify what you are going to do before doing it) has a greater chance of success than a poorly thought out plan.

Remember Me

Individuals, groups, departments, organizations, etc. perform work efforts.

A work effort has measurable results or goals. What is an example of a work effort with goals? The strategic plan for an organization is a perfect example. The mission, vision, direction, and goals for the organization are clearly established. The plan is then communicated to the organization, and management nurtures the plan and adjusts as time goes on.

Exercise

CSQ3® applies to any organization. As mayor of a city, assign two work efforts to your Police Department.

Loyal Subject is somewhat confused about the future talk. Loyal needs to put the ideas into everyday Land of Near language:

1. Which of the following is a work effort?

   A. Building a New School

   B. Bowing to a Noble

   C. Talking to the Blacksmith

   (Correct answer is A)

2. Loyal's friend, Good Friend, wants to make an investment, which of the following is a work effort?

   A. Giving money to the church

   B. Buying a Tavern

   C. Paying a kick back to a Noble

   (Correct answer is B)

3. The Province of Pain wants to make life in Pain less painful, which is a work effort?

   A. Eliminating hangings for one week

   B. Reducing the number of beatings for the month

   C. Planning a new Merchants Section in the province

(Correct answer is C)

Loyal is on track now... Back to future gaze...

Phases

A phase is an identifiable division of work activity in a work effort. There are five phases in every CSQ3® work effort. The phases are Concept (Big Picture), Structure (Framework), Detail (Fill in the Specifics), Implement (Make it Happen), and Operate (Manage the Results).

Break a Work Effort into Phases

One of the primary concerns about breaking-up a work effort into phases is that it will take more time. Nothing is further from the truth. The phases are progressive and objective looks at a work effort. Once the look is complete; move on to the next phase. There are no time limits on completing a phase. Some phases may take minutes others may take hours, days, months, or even years.

The breakup of CSQ3® work efforts into phases is based on the following principle: "Clearly establish what you are going to do, before doing it." It sounds so simple, yet how many times do we just quickly react to a given situation.

As shown in the Figure, there are 5 phases in the CSQ3® work flow methodology. If the first three phases are performed well, the odds for a highly successful work effort are greatly increased.

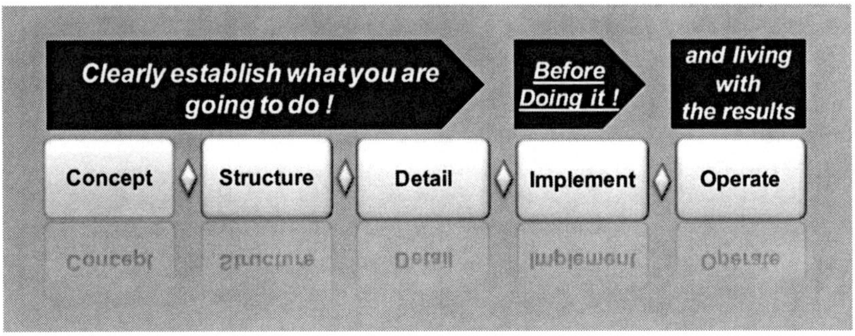

Figure 6

The objective of each phase is highlighted below:

- **Concept Phase** – Look at the Big Picture, increase and decrease the overall scope, look for show stoppers, and opportunities. The Concept Phase is the time for out-of-the-box thinking.
- **Structure Phase** – Establish the Framework; develop the main building blocks or principles of implementation.
- **Detail Phase** – Fill in the Specifics; develop a comprehensive implementation plan.
- **Implement Phase** – Make it Happen, buy the car; build the house.

- **Operate Phase** – Manage the Results; run the organization.

Concept Phase – "Big Picture"

The Concept Phase is the Big Picture. Increase and decrease the magnitude of the work effort scope. Make sure the work effort is solving the correct problem or aiming toward the right goal. Take the time to look at completely different alternatives.

In the Concept Phase, think out-of-the-box. Ask the questions: "What are the Show Stoppers to the work effort?" "What are the Opportunities related to the work effort?"

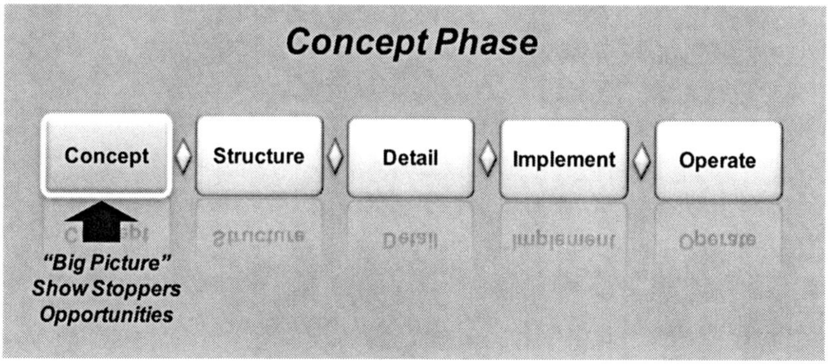

Figure 7

For example, a high school student's work effort is to get a car. What is a Concept Phase "Show Stopper"? No Money! What is a potential Concept Phase "Opportunity?" Uncle Laurence is buying a new car, and he wouldn't mind donating his old car to a needy high school student.

The CSQ3® Solution is applicable to any organization. Here are some examples of Show Stoppers and Opportunities for profit, non-profit, and government organizations.

Profit Organization

Assume the work effort is the building of a manufacturing plant that will produce nanotechnology products (manufacturing technology that will make most products lighter, stronger, cleaner, less expensive, or more precise). Initial discussions are focused on the manufacturing of nanotechnology solar cells. What's a potential show stopper or opportunity?

- **Show Stopper:** existing legal patents already cover the nanotechnology manufacturing process for solar cells and trying to get around the patents would not be possible.
- **Opportunity:** with a slight modification to the nanotechnology process, light weight bullet proof glass can be manufactured.

The new manufacturing plant will be designed to manufacture light weight bullet proof glass.

Non-Profit Organization

A charity wants to expand their services to the homeless. The work effort is to secure major sources of funding. Concept Phase discussions lead to the conclusion that corporate sponsorship is needed. What's a potential show stopper or opportunity?

- **Show Stopper:** the charter for the charity forbids direct corporate sponsorship.

- **Opportunity:** the charter does not forbid the charity from joining an association of charities. The association could go after corporate sponsorship and the charity would receive a percentage of the donations.

The charity decides to form an association with the purpose of obtaining major corporate donations. The organization develops the mission and vision for the "Association of Charities."

Government Organization

A City is planning the repair of high schools due to the availability of Federal funds. The work effort is to repair the high schools. What's a potential show stopper or opportunity?

- **Show Stopper:** the Federal funds are not available or have too many strings attached.

- **Opportunity:** there are additional repair projects that the city was planning to do.

The City decides to combine all repair projects into one repair work effort.

Exercise

Identify a past work effort where "When it was all over, you wished you would have done something completely different?"

Loyal Subject understands the idea of "Clearly establishing what you are going to do before doing it." Loyal has **not** done that on numerous occasions and, has suffered from the results.

Good Friend is considering the purchase of a Tavern. What should be considered in the Concept Phase?

- **Big Picture:** Go up and down a level of scope. For example, going up a level, consider investing in the Tavern and the restaurant next door; or going down a level of scope, instead of buying, lease the Tavern for a certain period of time.

- **Show Stopper:** The Noble will cut Good Friend's head off, if Good Friend buys the Tavern.

- **Opportunity:** Ask the Noble about a possible partnership, where they can purchase numerous Taverns.

Loyal is looking forward to Good Friend's potential Tavern investment. Back to future gaze…

Structure Phase – "Framework"

The Structure Phase is the "Skeleton" or the "Framework" of the implementation solution. The Structure Phase is the outline of what is to be implemented.

For example, the work effort is buying a house. Assuming the Country, State, and City decisions have been answered in the Concept Phase, what are some key Structure Phase decisions? Key Structure Phase decisions might include: inside the City limits or suburbs, number of bedrooms, minimum square feet, acceptable price range, school districts, potential job opportunities, etc. The Structure Phase would involve searching through the multiple listings and narrowing down the potential number of houses to a reasonable number.

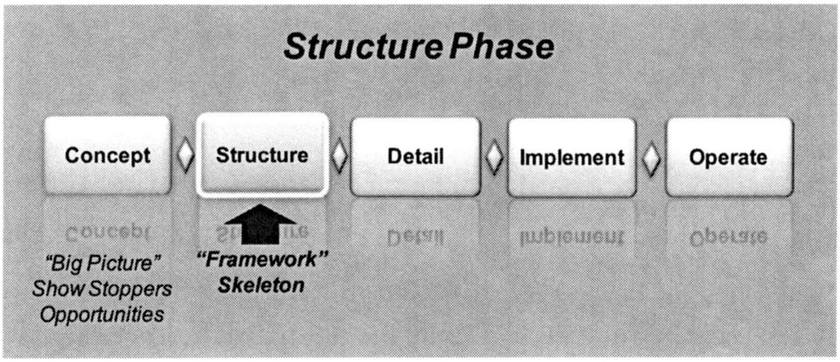

Figure 8

Continuing with the work effort examples...

Profit Organization

What's the "Framework" for the nanotechnology manufacturing plant? There will be two production lines with each line having the capability of producing one million square feet of nano-bullet-proof glass per year. The manufacturing complex will include four main processing buildings, an office building, and a research lab. An ultra-clean water supply of approximately 50,000 gallons per day is required for the manufacturing process.

Non-Profit Organization

What's the "Framework" for the Association of Charities? The framework is essentially the outline of the strategic plan for the association, which builds on the mission, vision and guiding principles established in the Concept Phase. The outline would include: legal structure, charitable services, marketing, membership, sponsorship, management of the association, work force, accounting requirements, ownership, Board of Directors, etc. In addition a listing of potential charities that maybe invited to join the association would be developed.

Government Organization

What's the "Framework" for the City of repair? Three high schools, a school bus terminal, and a City courthouse will be repaired. Repairs will include new roofs, windows, additional insulation, and new heating, ventilation, and air conditioning (HVAC) systems. In addition, state-of-the-art computing systems will be installed in all repaired buildings.

The Structure Phase is the outline of the work effort solution. The work effort is to build your dream house. How many bedrooms and bathrooms? What other items would you include?

Loyal understands the Structure Phase. The phase is similar to the main headings in an outline. Loyal decides that Good Friend needs help with the Tavern investment. There are actually two work efforts. One work effort is the investment in the Tavern. The second work effort is the refurbishment of the Tavern; if the Tavern is bought. With respect to the refurbishment work effort, Loyal has some items that need to be decided on in the Structure Phase.

The items include:

- How big is the bar?
- Are we going to serve snacks?
- How many people can the Tavern accommodate?
- Is the bar for Nobles or towns people?
- Do we have any entertainment?
- How many beer and ale taps? (It determines storage capacity.)

Detail Phase – "Fill In the Specifics"

In the Detail Phase, one needs to "Put the Meat on the Bones." "Fill in the Specifics."

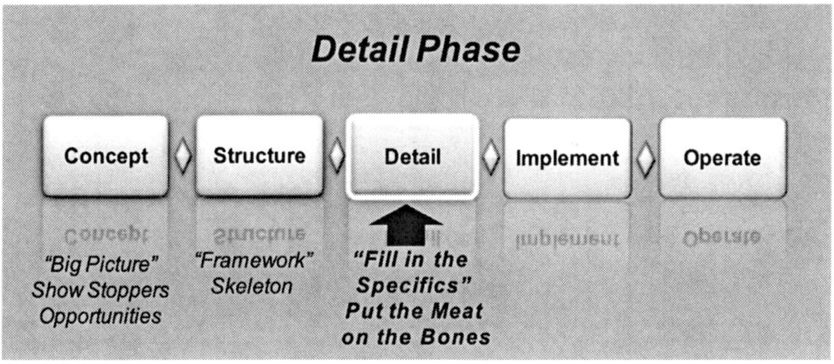

Figure 9

In buying a house, the Detail Phase would involve taking the multiple listings, and further narrowing down the list of potentials. Visiting neighborhoods and houses for sale would occur. As the potential list narrows, taxes, utility estimates, transportation needs, work and school considerations and the feel (intangibles) of the various houses come into play. In other words "Clearly establish what you are going to do."

Profit Organization

In the Detail Phase of the nanotechnology manufacturing complex, the layout of the entire facility, manufacturing diagrams, process diagrams, mechanical diagrams, equipment specifications, and construction specifications, etcetera are developed.

Non – Profit Organization

With respect to the Association of Charities, the details associated with each framework category are further developed. For example, the legal form of the association is established. Details related to Federal and State taxes are worked out. Accounting guidelines for accepting and reporting contributions are reviewed. Contract details with other Charities that may join the association are written. Marketing material is created. A targeted listing of charitable organizations is developed.

Government Organization

In the City with numerous repairs, the Detail Phase clearly states the repair requirements for each building. For example, what are the specifications for the new roofs? Each building is evaluated and an acceptable new roof design, with exact material specifications is provided. How many windows are to be replaced and what are the specifications for the new windows? What are the specifications for the new HVAC systems? The Detail Phase should include contracting specifics, inspection criteria, and acceptance/approval procedures.

Government Organization – Lump Sum Bid Example

Now, let's assume that the City wants to award the repair work to just one contractor, and the bid needs to be lump sum (one price for the work with minimal extra costs). The City hires an engineering firm to join the work effort team in order to help out with the Detail Phase work activities. The Detail Phase clearly establishes the design basis. Once the design basis is established, the City bids the work to several construction/repair contractors. The lump sum bids are submitted and the engineering firm evaluates the bids, finally recommending one contractor for the work. All of the above is performed in the Detail Phase. Hence, if City management approves moving forward with the work effort; costs and schedules are known, quality is built in by design, and implementation is expedited.

Exercise

Have you ever assigned work to a person in which you wished that you had provided more detailed instructions?

Loyal likes the Detail Phase. Loyal is checking out beer tap catalogues. If Good Friend decides to make the Tavern investment, Loyal will be at Good Friend's side.

Supreme Ruler checks in with Loyal Subject. Loyal quickly hides the catalogues. "Remember the Challenge" Supreme Ruler shouts.

Loyal goes back into future gaze…

Implement Phase – "Make It Happen"

In the Implement Phase, Make It Happen. Put the plan into effect; go after the major contract; construct the building; buy the car, etc.

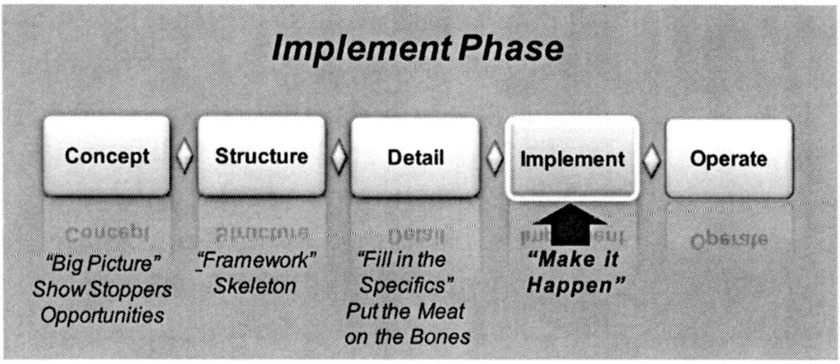

Figure 10

In the Implement Phase, the green light has been given to take action and/or to make significant commitments. With respect to the house example, an actual offer to buy a house would occur. The implementation of a negotiations plan would unfold. The initial offer might include the provision for an outside inspection company to inspect the house, etc. The inspection results would be useful in further negotiations. If the offer and negotiations are successful, the house is purchased in the Implement Phase.

Profit Organization

In the Implement Phase the nanotechnology manufacturing complex is built. Construction contracts are awarded, equipment purchased and installed, etc. Operations personnel are trained in preparation for start up.

Non – Profit Organization

In the Implement Phase, a core group of charitable organizations is contacted for possible inclusion in the Association of Charities. If the response is positive, the core group establishes the Association of Charities. If the response is negative, the work effort is killed.

Government Organization

In the Implement Phase, the City awarded the repair work to one lump sum contractor. The working relationship between the contractor and City is good. However, City personnel understand the Cost, Schedule, and Quality pressures of lump sum contracts and hires additional inspectors for each of the repair sites.

Exercise

The Implement Phase is the execution of the plan, communication of organizational direction, signing of major deals, etc. If the work effort is your retirement plan, what occurs? (make the investments, etc.)

Loyal is in high spirits… Good Friend bought the Tavern. The negotiations for the purchase of the Tavern were tough. However, Loyal Subject and Good Friend developed a well thought out plan and Good Friend breezed thru the formal negotiations. The Tavern will need refurbishment. Fortunately, Loyal has spent considerable time on that work effort.

Operate Phase – "Manage the Results"

In the Operate Phase, "Manage the Results;" run the organization; manage the contract; operate the facility; maintain the car, etc. With respect to buying a house, the Operate Phase represents ownership. Ownership includes maintaining the house, paying the mortgage, utilities, taxes, etc.

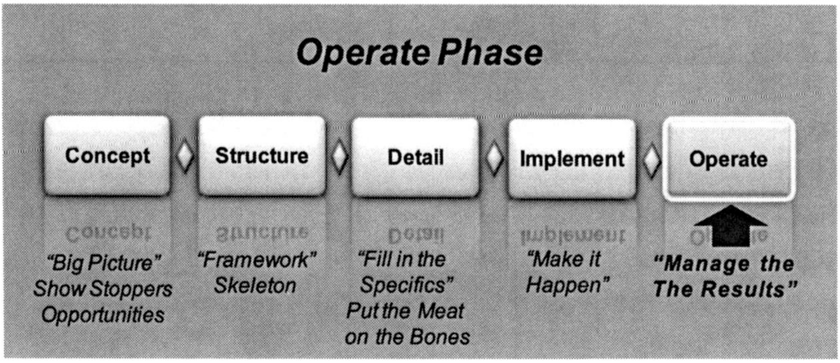

Figure 11

<u>*Profit Organization*</u>

Operating the nanotechnology manufacturing complex is an awesome responsibility and challenge. The potential technical, human resources and logistic problems are significant, especially when considering new technology.

Non – Profit Organization

In the Operate Phase of the Association of Charities, operations begin. Contracts with additional charities that want to join the association are signed. Corporate sponsorship is sought. Charitable projects are launched.

Government Organization

In the Operate Phase of the City Government repair work effort, punch list any items that need to be corrected; accept the work performed; and, hold the contractors liable for any workmanship or equipment warranties.

Exercise

The work effort is buying a house. What happens in the Operate Phase? (Maintain the house, pay taxes, etc.) What if you decide to put/build a gazebo in the back yard? (Launch a new work effort.)

Loyal needs to teach CSQ3® Fundamentals to the people of Near. Loyal remembers, "Clearly establish what you are going to do, before doing it."

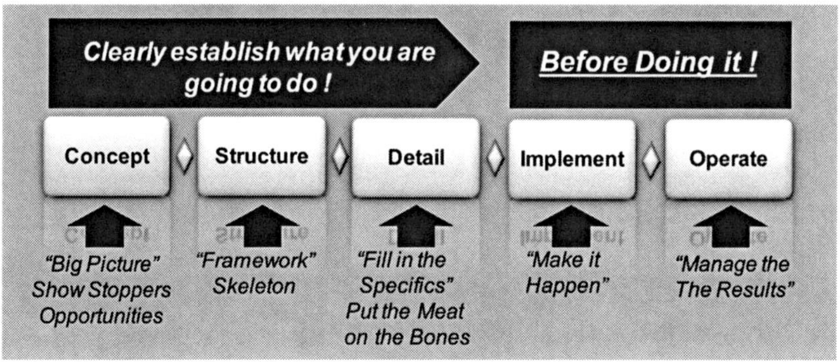

Figure 12

Loyal is extremely happy. Good Friend is now the operator of "The Tavern." Good Friend and Loyal couldn't think of an appropriate name, so they just called it "The Tavern."

Loyal goes back into future gaze…

What Occurs After Operate

What occurs after the Operate Phase? It depends on the work effort but, generally new work efforts are launched. With respect to buying a house, new work efforts would include: remodeling the kitchen, adding a patio, planting a garden, etc.

The nanotechnology manufacturing complex is ripe for additional work efforts. Some will be minor and some maybe major. For example, repairing a pump would be a minor work effort; increasing the production line efficiency by 25% would be a major work effort.

As mentioned, the Association of Charities begins its' operation, which includes: the signing up of new charitable organizations, obtaining sponsorship and funds, conducting charitable projects.

With respect to the City Government repair work effort, besides warranty issues, the work effort is complete. However, there would be additional work efforts related to normal building operations.

The following Mind Breaker was from a very unique consulting assignment, where the work flow process was utilized to improve the performance of a management team.

The work effort is to create a "High Performance Management Team". The work effort team is management. What is the objective and expected results from each phase? (Go thru each phase highlighting the hard points (authority, responsibility, etc.) and soft points (trust, being a human being, etc.).

While thinking about the "Mind Breaker," Loyal Subject has a brain freeze. Imagine Supreme Ruler and the nobility from all the provinces in the Land of Near getting together with the purpose of creating a high performance management team! Swords need to be banned because some nobles may not leave the hall…

Management Decision Points

Management Decision Points are located in between work effort phases. Management Decision Points are reviews between the work effort team and management.

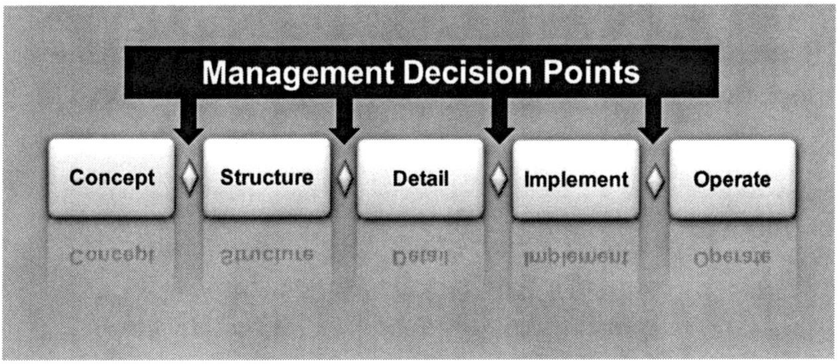

Figure 13

The management decision is simple, "Kill" the work effort or "Approve" the work effort to the next phase. In most situations, the "Kill" or "Approve" decision is made by the person or persons that have monetary or moral authority in the organization.

Note, the discussion on Management Decision Points relates to work efforts where there is a clear management structure. If there is not a clear management structure, use the terminology "Decision Points." A "Kill" or "Approve" decision still needs to be made. Hence, the person or persons that are performing the work effort should agree on how or who will make the decision at each Decision Point.

Management Needs Cost, Schedule, and Quality Information

What does management expect at a Management Decision Point? Management needs to know if the work effort team accomplished the objectives of the current phase, and if the work effort team recommends "Killing" or "Approving" the work effort. If the work effort team recommends "Approval," the requirements and the plans for the next phase need to be identified. Most importantly, management needs Cost, Schedule, and Quality information.

Exercise

A Decision Maker usually has monetary authority; but, also needs to communicate with work effort teams. In your organization, who should be the Decision Maker(s)?

Loyal Subject and the Supreme Ruler talk. The Supreme Ruler likes Management Decision Points. Breaking up a work effort into phases makes sense, and management involvement in between phases is an excellent idea. The Supreme Ruler can decide on the managers that will preside at Management Decision Points.

Supreme Ruler's eyes perked up a bit when the talk was about "Killing" work efforts but, Loyal Subject did not pursue the matter. Loyal goes back into future gaze...

Estimating Cost and Schedule

At a Management Decision Point the work effort team presents Cost, and Schedule information. Obviously, management would be interested in the cost for implementing a work effort, and the date when operations will begin. Consequently, at the end of the Concept, Structure, and Detail Phases a work effort team produces Cost and Schedule estimates. As shown in the figure, the range in estimates is +/- 40% for the Concept Phase; +/- 25% for the Structure Phase; and, +/- 15% for the Detail Phase.

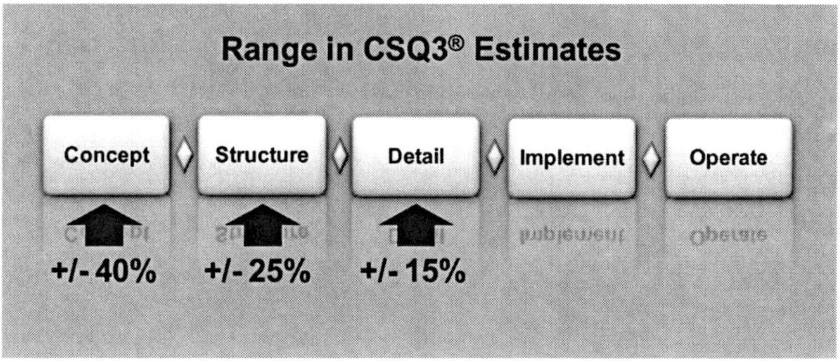

Figure 14

The range in accuracy helps work effort teams determine the work that needs to be performed in a phase. For example, in the Concept Phase the accuracy of the estimates is + /- 40%. A work effort team should only do enough work to develop a +/-40% estimate. Do not perform Structure Phase or Detail Phase work in the Concept Phase.

Let's assume the work effort is to buy a new car, and the buyers are a young couple with 2 children. What would the cost estimate for the Concept Phase look like?

Cost Estimate Concept Phase (+/- 40% Accuracy)

The Concept Phase is "Big Picture," "Show Stoppers" and "Opportunities." Although a performance sports car is really wanted, the Concept Phase results in the determination that a family car that will accommodate four people is the only choice. Research indicates that the average price for a family car with standard options is $30,000, which is in line with the work effort budget. Knowing $30,000 times 40% is $12,000; the range in car prices could be as low as $30,000 - $12,000 = $18,000 or as high as $30,000 + $12,000 = $42,000. Hence, the work effort will identify car models that meet any additional Concept Phase criteria and fits in the $18,000 to $42,000 price range. With such a large range, the work effort will probably not worry about extra options, taxes, warranties, dealer location, car color, cup holders, etc. The phase is focused on the "Big Picture." Let's assume that there are 10 automotive models that meet the Concept Phase criteria. What about the Structure Phase?

Exercise

At +/- 40% the Concept Phase estimates are similar to "Ball Park" estimates. Assume that the work effort is taking a vacation. What's the "Ball Park" Cost Estimate of your vacation?

Cost Estimate Structure Phase (+/- 25% Accuracy)

The Structure Phase establishes the "Framework" of the work effort. Let's assume the Structure Phase work effort produces the following criteria: family car, four full size adults, 30+ miles per gallon, four doors, high Safety rating, maximum stereo system (factory installed), dealer needs to be within 30 miles, etc. The Structure Phase identifies three acceptable car models. The average cost of the three models is $28,500 (25% of $28,500 is $7,125). The Structure Phase estimate has a range of $35,625 on the high side ($28,500 + $7,125 = $35,625) and $21,375 on the low side ($28,500 - $7,125 = $21,375). What about the cost estimate for the Detail Phase?

Cost Estimate Detail Phase (+/- 15% Accuracy)

In the Detail Phase, the work effort gets down to specifics. On each of the three car models, every option is identified. Factory suggested and dealer costs are obtained from published literature. The dealers are identified. Test drives of the three car models are made. One car model stands out as the winner. Taking into account all of the options, taxes, financing, discounts, etcetera the work effort estimates the drive home cost to be $29,550 +/- 15%, which calculates to $33,982 on the high side and $25,118 on the low side. With costs identified, the work effort approaches the Management Decision Point between the Define and Implement Phases. (Note: it is assumed that the young couple has the funds to purchase the car; hence, they are making the decision at the Management Decision Point). In the Implement Phase if negotiations are successful, a car would be purchased.

Note, with respect to cost estimates, management is interested in the cost to implement a work effort. Except for valid punch list items, Operating Phase costs (operations, maintenance, etcetera) and operational revenue are not included in the cost estimate of a work effort.

Remember Me

The Cost Estimate of a Work Effort does not include Operating Phase Costs or Revenues.

Estimating Schedules

The above discussion is on costs "What about schedules?," "What are schedule estimates related to?" Schedule estimates always relate to the start of the Operate Phase. Schedule and Cost estimates have the same range in accuracy. The Concept Phase is +/- 40 %; the Structure Phase is +/- 25%; and, the Detail Phase is +/- 15%.

In the car example, let's assume that the work effort is nearing the end of the Concept Phase. A schedule estimate is needed. Assume the following durations:

- Structure Phase 5 days

- Detail Phase 15 days
- Implement Phase 3 days
- The total duration is 5 + 15 + 3 = 23 days.

With an accuracy of +/- 40%, that would be 23 + (.40 x 23) = 32 days on the high side; and, 23 – (.40 x 23) = 14 days on the low side.

Also note, as shown in the figure, at the start of the Operate Phase the Actual Cost and Actual Schedule of a work effort can be determined.

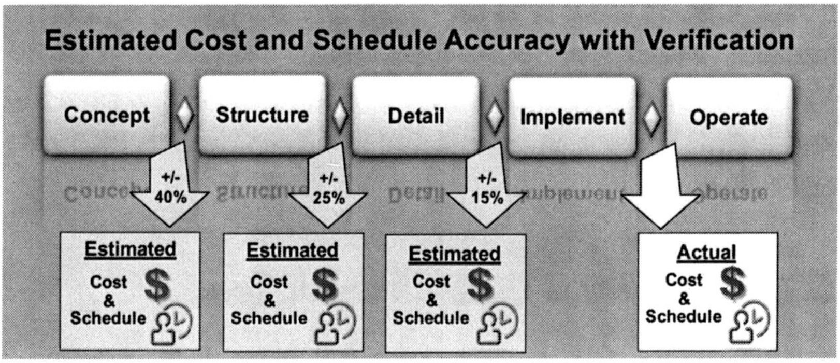

Figure 15

The Schedule Estimate of a Work Effort relates to the start of the Operate Phase.

Loyal Subject likes the correlation of phase activity to the given estimate ranges. Loyal remembers growing up and the agony of figuring out math problems with grandfather's abacus. If only the teacher would have accepted Concept Phase estimates...

Loyal feels comfortable with explaining Cost and Schedule to the populous of Near. When a custom-made saddle is ordered, a person wants to know the cost, and when it will be ready. Loyal goes back to future gaze....

Quality – Estimating Value

Besides Cost and Schedule information a work effort team presents Quality information at a Management Decision Point. CSQ3® Quality is the "Delivery of Actual Value" and the "Making of Sound Decisions." With respect to Value, Value estimates are made in the Concept, Structure, and Detail Phases. Actual Value is determined in the Operate Phase.

CSQ3® Quality is the Delivery of Value

CSQ3® Quality is estimating and delivering Value. Well, what is Value? If a person goes to the bank and can get a 1% or a 5% interest rate on their savings, which is better? Obviously, the higher return is better. Value is used to rank one work effort over another. CSQ3® Value is always measured in financial terms.

Use Return on Investment (ROI) to Estimate Value

The easiest way to establish Value is to calculate Return on Investment (ROI) which equals (Revenues – Investment) / (Investment). Note: in the ROI calculations the time value of money is usually taken into account ($1000 today is worth less in the future). For simplicity, the Value examples do not take into account the discounting of cash flow over time.

Let's take another car example (buying and then leasing out a car). Assume we buy a car at an Investment Cost of $500 per month. We then lease the car for Revenue of $600 per month. Only consider 1 year, assume the interest rate is 0%, and do not take into account tax credits, etcetera the ROI = (($600 x 12) – ($500 x 12)) / ($500 x 12) = .20 or a 20% Return on Investment. Value is equal to Revenue minus Investment divided by the Investment.

Remember Me

Value = ROI = (Revenues – Investment) / Investment

Note, revenues may also include intangibles or goodwill. However, the intangibles or goodwill must be reasonable, measurable, and applicable to other work efforts in the organization.

Soul Searcher

Everything has a "Value". How would you estimate the effects of an environmental disaster or the loss of just one human life? (This is an item that can be discussed and argued for days. Realistically the common denominator is money.)

Range in Value Estimate per Phase

What's the range in estimating Value, and when is Actual Value determined? Value estimates are in the same range as Cost and Schedule: +/- 40% in the Concept Phase; +/- 25% in the Structure Phase; and, +/- 15% in the Detail Phase.

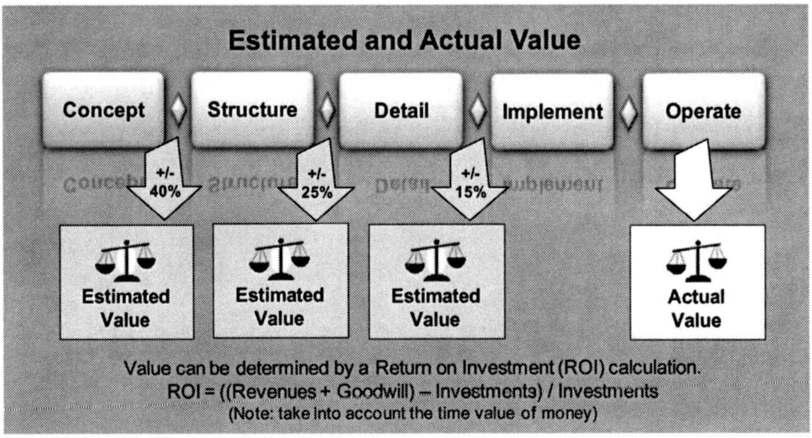

Figure 16

Actual Value is determined in the Operate Phase once stable and predictable operational generated Revenue can be determined. Comparing Estimated Value to Actual Delivered Value is a critical CSQ3® criteria in determining the overall performance of an organization.

The Value Estimate of a Work Effort does include Operating Phase Costs and Revenues.

Assume that you are the mayor of a City. One work effort is the construction of a new access road to a future subdivision. Another work effort is the installation of free and fast internet service in the downtown shopping district. Since the City has limited funds, what work effort do you choose? What information do you need?

Remember Me

Estimates have the following Accuracy:
+/- 40% Concept Phase
+/- 25% Structure Phase
+/- 15% Detail Phase

Exercise

Concept Phase estimates are similar to "Ball Park" estimates. Assume that the work effort is taking a vacation. What's the "Ball Park" Value Estimate of your vacation?

Loyal Subject is a little perplexed about Value but, certainly understands the need to compare Estimated Value to Actual Delivered Value. Estimated Values are needed by management at Management Decision Points. If the Estimated Value is too low (in comparison with other work efforts), a work effort maybe "Killed." However, if the work effort team lies and claims a very high Estimated Value; and then, Actual Value (Operate Phase) is found to be considerably less, the work effort team may get their heads chopped off.

Good Friend stopped by to tell Loyal about some recent wild escapades at The Tavern. Apparently some nobles visited The Tavern and a raucous ensued. Loyal reflects about the conversation and then goes back to future gaze…

Quality - Making Sound Decisions

Besides Value, CSQ3® Quality is the "Making of Sound Decisions." How does a work effort team go about making sound decisions? What's the CSQ3® methodology? The following is a methodology that has worked with work effort teams throughout the world. The methodology is the building of a Decision Quality Table.

Building a Decision Quality Table

The steps to building a Decision Quality Table are summarized in the following figure.

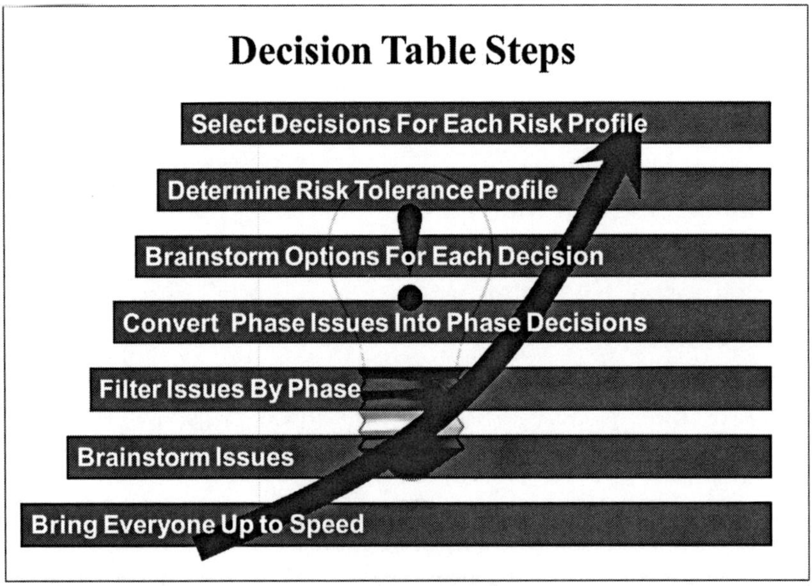

Figure 17

A Decision Quality Table is applicable to any phase. It is assumed that the core work effort team is formed and any personnel new to the team have settled in. The table is created as early as possible in a phase and is generally developed with the entire team in a workshop atmosphere. The purpose of creating the table is to establish the key decisions that the work effort team needs to make in the current phase.

First, Bring Everyone Up to Speed

The first part of the workshop is the sharing of information where all work effort team members and workshop participants are brought up to speed. Besides work effort teams members, other participants might include experts from within the organization, experts from outside of the organization, management, and/or facilitators. The sharing of information is generally by way of presentations. Work effort leaders provide background on the scope of the work effort, current phase, and key work effort accomplishments from the previous phases, as applicable. Next, key functional leaders in the work effort or individual team members provide presentations in their areas of expertise or participation. The purpose is to bring everyone up to the same level playing field.

Second, Brainstorm Issues

The next part is to brainstorm issues. There are no wrong or inappropriate issues. However, every issue must be in the form of a question and only one issue per question. Issues might include: Where will the facility be located?

Who will sign the contract? What's the mission of the task force? What's the voltage of the electrical system?

Perform the brainstorming as quickly as possible. The issues should be focused on the work effort. Issues related to any phase are appropriate.

If there is a pause in the action, throw out key words related to topics that may not have been touched such as, competition, regulations, financial, risk, etc. In addition, if there are departments or areas that are not represented, cover those areas, i.e. human resources, information technology, legal, accounting, operations, etc.

Third, Filter Issues by Phase

Filter the brainstormed issues by phase. Separate the issues into three categories: Previous Phase or Phases, Current Phase, and Future Phase or Phases.

Do not waste time on issues related to a previous phase or phases. Tell the workshop participants that it was covered in previous work or is outside of the workshop scope. If need be, take up the discussion after the workshop.

Do not waste time on issues related to a future phase or phases. If the work effort gets "Killed" the future phase issues won't matter. Concentrate only on the issues related to the current phase!!

Remember Me

To determine if an issue is relevant to the current phase, ask the question "Would the issue effect the range in estimation accuracy?" (+/- 40% Concept, +/- 25% Structure, +/- 15% Detail).

Fourth, Convert Current Phase Issues into Phase Decisions

Convert current phase issues into current phase decisions. There are generally numerous issues related to each decision. The decision should reflect the general nature of the issues. The decision should be one or two words and placed in the top row of a Decision Table. Leave the first column of the table blank.

Normally, in a Decision Quality Workshop the current phase issues are separated into functional areas. The larger group is then broken down into their respective areas of expertise. The personnel assigned to particular areas will then review the provided issues and convert the issues into decisions.

As an example, the work effort is buying a new car and the following Detail Phase issues have been raised: Should we have a High Definition radio? What video systems are available? Do we need GPS? What about leather seats? Is there a larger engine?

The Detail Phase decisions for the above issues would be: Audio System, Video System, Navigation System, Interior Seats, Engine Options, respectively, as shown in the figure.

New Car Decision Table

— ...rollable & Risk Mitigation Decisions for the Current ... —

Risk Tolerance	Audio System	Video System	Navigation System	Interior Seats	Engine Options
	Option	Option	Option	Option	Option
	Option	Option	Option	Option	Option
	Option	Option	Option	Option	Option
	Option	Option	Option	Option	Option
	Option	Option	Option	Option	Option

Figure 18

Fifth, Brainstorm Options for Each Decision

For each decision brainstorm all reasonable and achievable options. Options should be unique and distinct from one another. Identify, roughly 4-6 options for each decision, if possible. Potential decision options for the new car example are shown in the figure below.

New Car Decision Table

— Controllable & Risk Mitigation Decisions for the Current Phase —

Risk Tolerance	Audio System	Video System	Navigation System	Interior Seats	Engine Options
	None	None	None	Standard	V6
	Standard	In Dash	Factory GPS	Leather	V8
	HD Radio	Overhead	Non-Factory GPS	Standard w Heating & Cooling	Hybrid
	HD Radio MP3, USB	Head Rest		Leather w Heating & Cooling	All Electric
	HD 1000 Watt Speakers	Universal Screen			

Figure 19

Note, decision options are normally identified by the respective functional personnel. Do not throw out wild options.

In fact, encourage wild options as long as they are reasonable and achievable. The purpose of the Decision Table is to identify critical phase decisions and all of the associated decision options.

Sixth, Determine Risk Tolerance

If a work effort team utilizes the phased approach, interacts with management, and makes sound decisions, the probability for a successful work effort is high. Consequently, the steps are in place for success. A critical variable is how much risk are you willing to take?

For example, if the work effort is your retirement plan, the amount of risk that you are willing to take will significantly affect the decisions that you make. If you have a conservative (low) risk tolerance, the majority of your investments would probably be in bonds. If you have a high risk tolerance (willing to take greater risks for higher rewards), the majority of your investment would favor stocks.

In a Decision Quality Workshop the entire team generally participates in the discussion on risk tolerance. The discussions can become time consuming. Fortunately, for most work efforts, only one risk profile is necessary. The Normal risk profile is a reflection on what the organizational culture would identify as an acceptable risk for the given work effort. It may be a feeling; it may be a reflection on what happens if things go bad; it may be based on acceptable financial parameters and numeric probabilities, etc. Establish the risk tolerance profile or profiles for the work effort.

Exercise

What is your "Normal" Risk Tolerance with respect to making investments?

Finally, Select Decisions for Each Risk Tolerance Profile

A decision table can have more than one risk profile. For each risk profile, go through the decision table, and select the appropriate decisions. Some decisions will be the same, some will be different.

If there are multiple risk tolerance profiles, the work effort team is then faced with the additional burden of determining the best profile. In the case where there are multiple risk tolerance profiles, use economics to determine the risk – reward relationship and the best profile.

In the car example, let's assume the person looking to buy the new car has no debts, no children, and just landed a great paying job after finishing college. What would the Decision Table for buying a new car look like?

Based on an assumed normal risk profile, the chosen decisions are highlighted in the figure on the next page.

New Car Decision Table

Controllable & Risk Mitigation Decisions for the Current Phase

Risk Tolerance	Audio System	Video System	Navigation System	Interior Seats	Engine Options
Normal	None	None	None	Standard	V6
	Standard	In Dash	Factory GPS	Leather	V8
	HD Radio	Overhead	Non-Factory GPS	Standard w Heating & Cooling	Hybrid
	HD Radio MP3, USB	Head Rest		Leather w Heating & Cooling	All Electric
	HD 1000 Watt Speakers	Universal Screen			

Figure 20

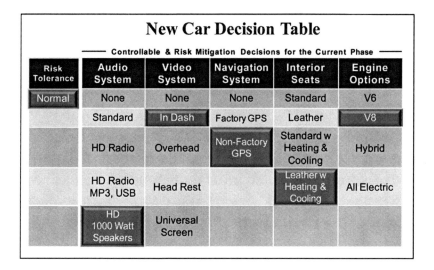

Decision Selection Streamlines Phase Activity

The making of sound decisions is applicable to every phase. Most decisions can be decided in a Decision Quality Workshop. Some decisions may require additional reflection, consultation with management, or risk mitigation calculations. However, making work effort decisions as early as possible in a phase, reduces work and simplifies the identification of tasks and activities that are necessary to complete the current phase.

Exercise

Your work effort is going on vacation (Concept Phase). Brainstorming issues have lead to the following two decisions: Location and Duration. What are the possible decision options for each?

Loyal Subject understands the importance of making sound decisions. Getting a work effort team together with the purpose of making decisions, focuses the team and eliminates unnecessary work.

Supreme Ruler stops by and Loyal Subject relates the steps for developing a Decision Table. Supreme Ruler is very interested. Besides the actual decisions and chosen path, the Supreme Ruler asked numerous questions about determining "Normal" risk tolerance and what is done to minimize risks when work effort risks are identified.

Does Loyal Subject have an understanding of CSQ3® Fundamentals? Is Loyal ready to complete Challenge #1?

Supreme Ruler puts Loyal to the test!

CSQ3® Fundamentals Test

1. How many phases are there in a work effort?

    A. One

    B. Two

    C. Four

    D. Five

2. The work effort is to buy a horse. In what phase is the horse actually purchased?

    A. Operate

    B. Detail

    C. Implement

    D. Structure

3. The saying "Clearly Establish what you are going to do" is associated with which phases?

    A. Implement

    B. Concept

    C. Detail

    D. Structure

4. "Doing It" in non guttural terms is associated with what phase?

    A. Structure

    B. Implement

    C. Concept

    D. Detail

5. Management options at a Management Decision Point are:

    A. Delay the work effort

    B. Kill the work effort

    C. Approve the work effort

    D. Let the work effort team decide

6. Cost, Schedule, and Quality are CSQ3® pillars. What is Quality?

    A. Maximizing Revenue

    B. Minimizing Costs

    C. Making Sound Decisions

    D. Delivering Actual Value

7. In the Return On Investment (ROI) equation, Revenue is included. What about a work effort that includes helping the sick?

   A. Too bad

   B. Include Intangibles in the Revenue term

   C. Substitute Costs into the equation

   D. Divide Revenue by the current interest rate

8. In the Structure Phase, the accuracy of the schedule estimate is :

   A. +/- 15%

   B. +/- 40%

   C. +/- 25%

   D. The same as the Value estimate

9. Creating a Decision Table includes the following steps:

   A. Brainstorming Issues

   B. Filtering Issues by phase

   C. Converting Issues Into Decisions

   D. Developing Decision Options

10. The name of The Tavern that Good Friend purchased is called:

    A. The Tavern

    B. The Place

    C. The Bar

    D. Ned's (Good Friend once had a wonderful dog named Ned)

1) D; 2) C; 3) B, C, D; 4) B; 5) B, C; 6) C, D; 7) B; 8) C, D;
9) A, B, C, D; 10) A

Loyal Subject has gone throughout the Land of Near teaching the Fundamentals of CSQ3® to the Populous. The Populous believe in Loyal's teachings. The Supreme Ruler has claimed that Loyal Subject has completed the 1st Challenge with flying colors!!

The 2nd Challenge will be more formidable!

Challenge #2: Taking On the Nobles of Intellectus, Thunder, and Pain (Teaching CSQ3® Optimum)

The 2nd Challenge is to implement a work effort system that will contain all key organizational work efforts in the Land of Near, simplify their management, and improve their performance. Supreme Ruler is asking for a lot but, Loyal Subject has the ability of "future gaze," where Loyal can see into the future. The Land of Near contains numerous provinces and the populous is large. Loyal sees that one day everyone in the land will be saying "We are performing, the Right Work, at the Right Time, with the Right People." Loyal needs to implement CSQ3® Optimum in the Land of Near.

On key work efforts, work efforts that have a significant effect on the people of Near, the Supreme Ruler uses the following provinces:

Intellectus: The province determines what needs to be done.

Thunder: The province implements key work efforts.

Pain: The province operates all key work efforts in the Land of Near.

Each province is like an island unto itself. Thick and tall walls are built. (The provinces represent departments in a typical organization).

Figure 21

Supreme Ruler is furious with the Provinces of Intellectus, Thunder, and Pain. With respect to key work efforts, Costs are too high, Schedules are too long, and Quality is non-existent. The Land of Near is not competitive with the outside world!

Loyal is very knowledgeable on CSQ3® Fundamentals. Using work effort fundamentals with the populous has produced excellent results. Can we utilize the same fundamentals on key work efforts?

With future gaze ability Loyal finds out that the answer is yes and no. Yes, CSQ3® Fundamentals apply. No, there are additional steps. Some of the steps relate to additional work that key work effort teams need to perform. However, most of the additional steps relate to the overall governance of the CSQ3® Optimum system. CSQ3® Optimum is an overall organizational work flow system. All key work efforts in the organization (which includes all multi-department work efforts) are contained in CSQ3® Optimum. The additional steps are as follows:

- Include Key Work Efforts
- Establish Scope
- Empower Teams
- Assign Resources
- Track Responsibility
- Report Using Execution Plus®
- Emphasis Management Decision Points
- Manage the CSQ3® Optimum Three Level (Strategic, Major Commercial, and Project) System

Loyal understands that the Challenge seems daunting. However, Loyal already has most of the needed knowledge. Imagine a work flow system that is applicable to every key work effort in the Land of Near.

Loyal decides to learn more about CSQ3® Optimum.

Loyal goes back into future gaze …

Include Key Work Efforts

CSQ3® methodology applies to any work effort from repairing a pump to establishing a strategic plan for a multinational organization. Obviously it would be impractical to include every work effort in an organization. So, what work efforts should be included in an organizational work flow system?

Start-up or very small organizations can be a lot of fun. Everyone knows everyone, and for the most part the good of the organization is the primary motivation.

Small organizations become larger, forming departments, divisions, sectors, etc. Walls are put up, kingdoms are built. Obtaining power can become more important than the good of the organization itself. Work efforts that require multi-department input are ripe for failure. From an individual department's perspective, a work effort might be classified as a complete success. From an overall organizational viewpoint, the discontinuity in work flow, and resulting work effort solution can be sub-optimal at best.

Don't get me wrong, departments and larger entities are important to an organization. The organizational entities should be "Centers of Knowledge" in their areas of expertise and responsibility. They train personnel, and provide critical support to the organization.

With respect to the CSQ3® Optimum work flow system, include all key organizational work efforts:

- Include department work efforts that are designated by management to be significant to the organization.

- For example, a new research work effort may have a small budget but, the potential results could be extremely beneficial to the organization.

- Include all work efforts that involve multiple departments or organizational entities.

    - For example, a division (an organizational entity with multiple departments) is going to build a new multi-state distribution system. The system will include warehouses, truck routes, and cost millions of dollars. Other divisions may launch similar work efforts.

Exercise

Which of the following work efforts would you enter into the CSQ3® Optimum organizational work flow system? (Assume the organization has a central design department and manufacturing plants throughout the world)

• Filing an order at one of the manufacturing plants (no)

• Replacing an electric motor in one of the production lines (no)

• Making minor modifications to one of the production lines (no, assuming manufacturing plant personnel have the skill sets)

• Making major modifications to one of the production lines (yes, the central design department as well as other departments need to be involved)

Supreme Ruler and Loyal Subject talk. Supreme Ruler understands the need to have work efforts that travel from one department to the next entered into the system. Supreme Ruler also understands the need for organizational oversight of the work flow system.

Supreme Ruler is involved with funding work efforts. If potential work efforts were submitted in a similar fashion, Supreme Ruler or a designate could review the work efforts in an expedited manner. The review could also point out similar work efforts that when combined could provide a greater benefit to the entire Land of Near.

Loyal Subject goes back into future gaze…

Establish Scope

The ideas for a great work effort can come from anyone in the organization but, management needs to review and fund all work efforts. Management has the fiscal responsibility and experience to determine which organizational entities need to be involved. Establishing the scope for any work effort is pretty simple. Before launching a new work effort, management should answer the following three questions:

1. **What is the work effort going to do?**

2. **Why are we doing it?**

3. **What does success look like?**

Scope Magnitude

With respect to the first question (What is the work effort going to do?), management should go up and down a magnitude in scope. For example, a knowledge management data base will be developed for use by the engineering and human resource departments in the New York and Chicago offices. Going up a magnitude, the organizational work effort scope might include a knowledge management database for all departments or all offices. The increase in scope may also include the combination of a knowledge management database with other new systems, etc. Going down a magnitude in scope, might result in the database implementation in only one location or the changing of the work effort to a departmental work effort which would not have to be included in the CSQ3® Optimum work flow system.

As another example, a department has decided that a new accounting work effort is appropriate. Is the new accounting work effort applicable to one department, numerous departments, or the entire organization? Management should go up and down a magnitude in work effort scope in order to determine which organizational entities will be involved and if the work effort should enter the CSQ3® Optimum work flow system.

Organizational Alignment

With respect to the second question (Why are we doing it?), a work effort needs organizational alignment. For example, implementation of the knowledge management database is in line with the organizational strategy for improving the intellectual memory, focus, and productivity of personnel (in other words, install the knowledge database so that personnel will quit making the same mistakes over and over again…). The knowledge database work effort is in alignment with the strategic direction of the organization.

Measurable and Tangible Results

With respect to the third question (What does success look like?), management should require measurable and tangible results. For example, in the knowledge database work effort: The response time for searching the database should be less than three seconds. Knowledge management information will be automatically entered into the database, etc.

In addition, Cost, Schedule, and Quality criteria can always be used as measurements of success. For example the Return on Investment (ROI) should not be less than 12%.

> **Exercise**
>
> ***List several bullet points of success for the following work effort: You form a non-profit charity to help people in your community. In three years time, what are your success measures?***

Loyal Subject likes the simplicity yet power of the three questions used to establish a work effort. Supreme Ruler can scan work effort scopes to make sure that the right work is being performed and that the right work efforts are entered into the work flow system.

What about the Provinces of Intellectus, Thunder, and Pain? The Provinces strive for control and power! How do we bypass their negative actions?

Loyal Subject goes back into future gaze…

Empower Teams

Allow all work effort teams to be in control of their own destiny. Take the political and control power away from departments (or larger organizational entities), and let the work effort teams manage their own work efforts. Generally, due to the importance of a work effort, the work effort team will be composed of personnel from numerous departments. In addition, most assigned personnel will be full time team members or will allocate the majority of their time to the work effort.

In most cases, the magnitude of work in a key organizational work effort is substantial. Unleash the power of human drive and initiative! Let the workers control their own destiny! Empower Work Effort Teams! The culture of the entire organization will change!

Exercise

Assume that you are one of the leaders in a work effort. What does "Control your own destiny" mean to you and to the rest of the team?

Loyal Subject likes the idea! Gosh, that will certainly kick the Nobles in the Back End!! Imagine personnel from Intellectus, Thunder, and Pain working together in all 5

Phases: Concept, Structure, Detail, Implement, and Operate.

Wait a second. There are Management Decision Points between each phase. Absolutely, management initially sets the scope of a work effort; lets the work effort team manage the phase work; and then, decides if the work effort should continue at a Management Decision Point. Management is not burdened with the day to day activities of the work effort. The work effort team is fired up, because they are in control of their own destiny. The work effort team has the opportunity to shine or fail.

In reality, there is a balance. The manager or managers that will be involved in making the decision at a Management Decision Point are interested in the work effort. The work effort team is interested in keeping management informed.

So who decides on the manager(s) at a Management Decision Point? It is up to individual organizations and their governance procedures.

Loyal Subject goes back into future gaze...

Assign Resources

Management is responsible for the running of the organization, which includes the assignment of resources to new and ongoing work efforts. Resources are all inclusive, such as financial, work office space, personnel assignments, etc.

Note, automating parts or the entire CSQ3® Optimum work flow system is possible. As an example, let's take a look at the potential assignment of work effort personnel.

A typical CSQ3® Optimum work effort team is composed of personnel from multiple organizational entities (departments). The overall scope of the work is known. Specific skill requirements and additional specifications are a function of the current work effort phase. Hence, the skill sets for personnel working in the Concept phase will probably vary from the skills sets of personnel working in the Implement phase.

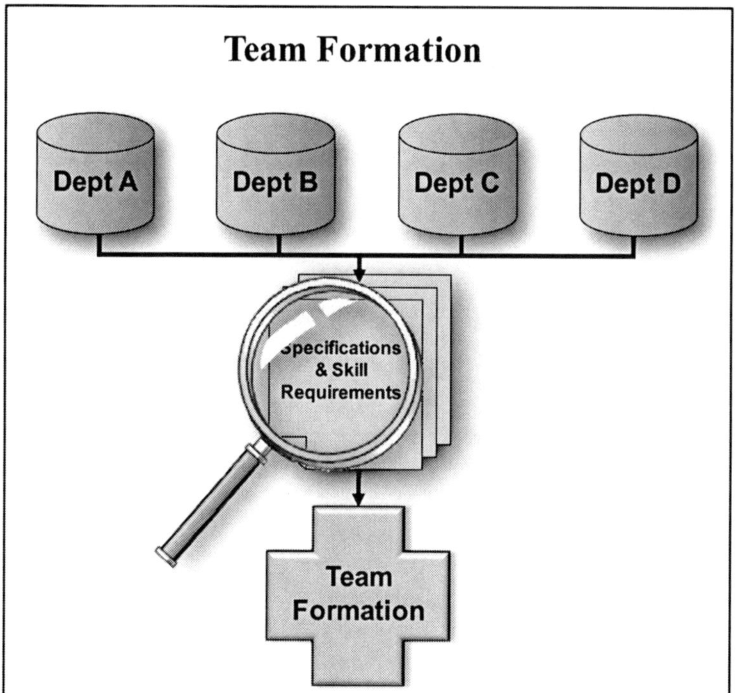

Figure 22

Team formation items for both the work effort leadership team and work effort team members are highlighted in the figure. The items include establishing the job requirements, searching for candidates, and then bringing the team members on board.

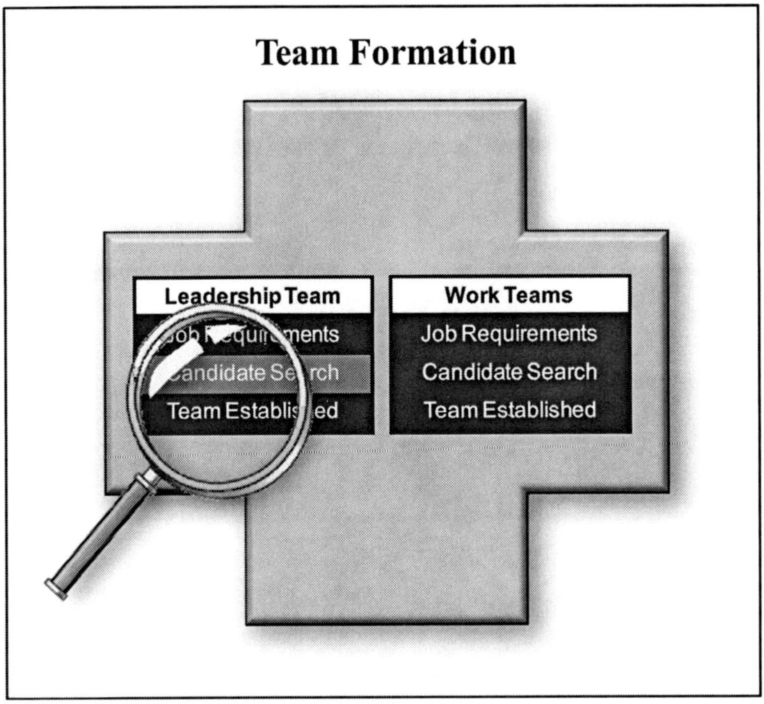

Figure 23

At the beginning of each phase, management or the work effort team leader develops personnel specifications and requirements. The personnel requests are sent to the appropriate departments for fulfillment. Skill set requests could lead to specific candidacy information, as shown in the figure on the next page. Matching candidate strengths to needed phase-specific team requirements could be a potential competitive advantage.

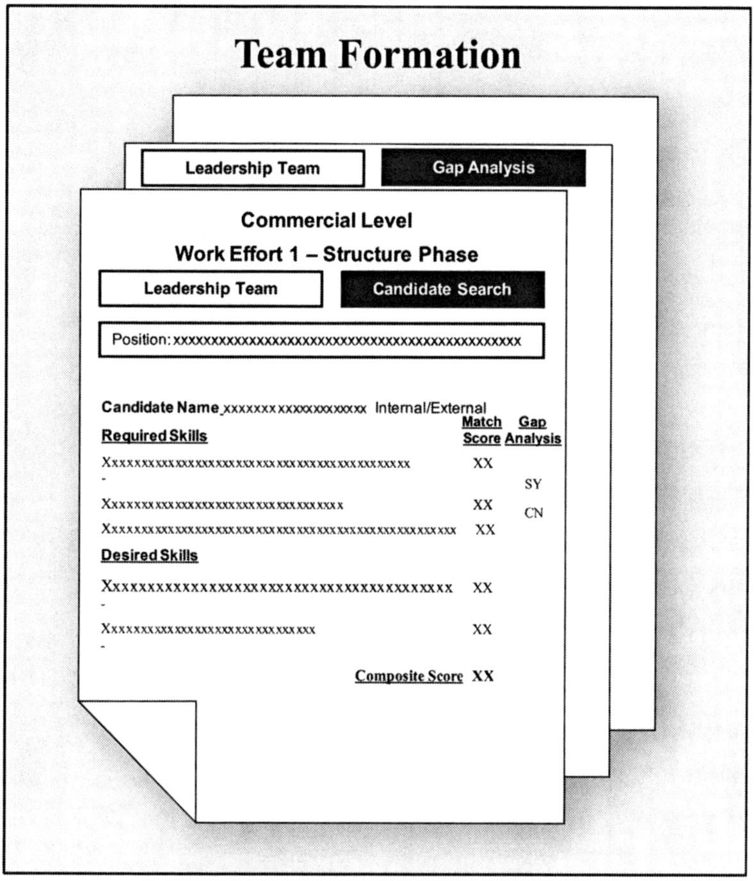

Figure 24

Departments are Centers of Knowledge. Departments provide personnel with functional expertise, additional support services, and management experience. CSQ3® Optimum requires the assignment of department personnel directly to empowered work effort teams. Department management is still responsible for the functional actions and decisions of the personnel that they provide to work effort teams. Consequently, the ability to manage an organization by the creation of departments is maintained; the inefficiencies created by running work efforts thru multiple departments is eliminated; and, the experience of department management in creating Centers of Knowledge is still incorporated.

Exercise

Getting the best qualified people on a work effort team has a lot of advantages. In your organization, how would you streamline the selection process for work effort team members?

Loyal Subject is starting to see how all the pieces might come together. Loyal recalls the teachings on how to create a Decision Table. There was brainstorming and focusing and refocusing with options leading to a path and direction with normal risk tolerance. (Loyal may need to review that section again).

Without going into a lot of detail, Loyal needs to know what are the CSQ3® Optimum changes to the creation of a Decision Table?

Loyal goes back into future gaze....

Track Responsibility

The easiest way to track responsibility is to capture Decision Table information. Decision Tables are required for the first four phases, and is recommended for the Operate phase. The tables are useful to teams performing similar work efforts and, the tables are useful in the appraisal of the work effort itself.

Advanced Decision Tables

Work effort teams make decisions. Critical work effort decisions are captured in a Decision Table. In order to simplify future appraisals, every decision in a work effort's Decision Table should be identified with a responsible department and functional group. For clarification, the department maybe Engineering, and the functional group within the department might be Electrical Engineering. In other organizations, the department may be Electrical Engineering with a functional group being Instrumentation. The intent is to track responsibility for decisions made by a work effort team.

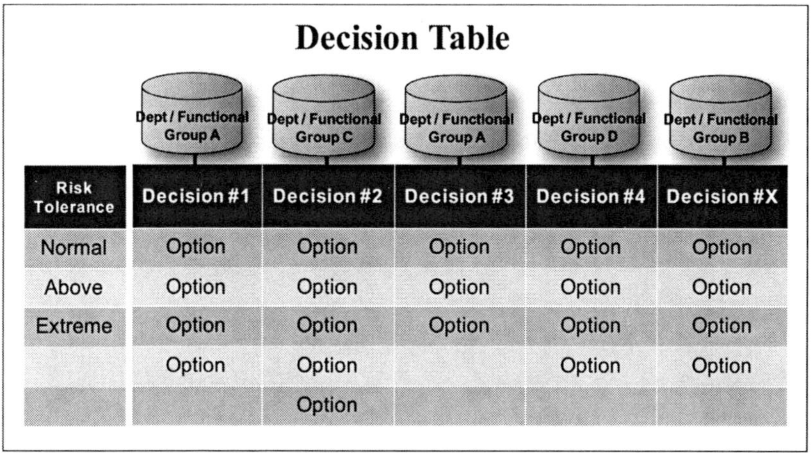

Figure 25

Include tracking information as part of or as an attachment to the Decision Table.

Note when a Decision Table is created by a work effort team, the direct representatives of all the affected departments may not be present. Moreover, work effort team members with some but, perhaps limited knowledge will represent a department. The information in the Decision Table will be used to appraise the performance of the work effort team and the departments in an organization. It is up to the work effort team members and the managers of the various departments to be aware of the decisions being made by work effort teams. There is a balance. The work effort team is in control of their own destiny but, departments train work effort team members and hence have a degree of accountability.

Track Risk

The first column in the Decision Table relates to an organization's Risk Tolerance. In non-critical work efforts a classification of "Normal" is acceptable. However, in critical work efforts it is common for work effort teams to increase or decrease the amount of risk. Generally, more risk (less conservative) more reward (ROI); less risk (more conservative) less reward. Consequently, the Decision Table should reflect the different Risk Tolerances established by a work effort team.

For example, assume a work effort team has identified three Risk Tolerance Profiles: Normal, Above, and Extreme. Normal represents the organization's normal risk tolerance for their work effort. Above represent actions that would lead to a higher ROI, and Extreme would represent actions or a direction that would lead to an even higher Return On Investment. Decisions based on each risk tolerance are then chosen by the work effort team, as illustrated in the figure.

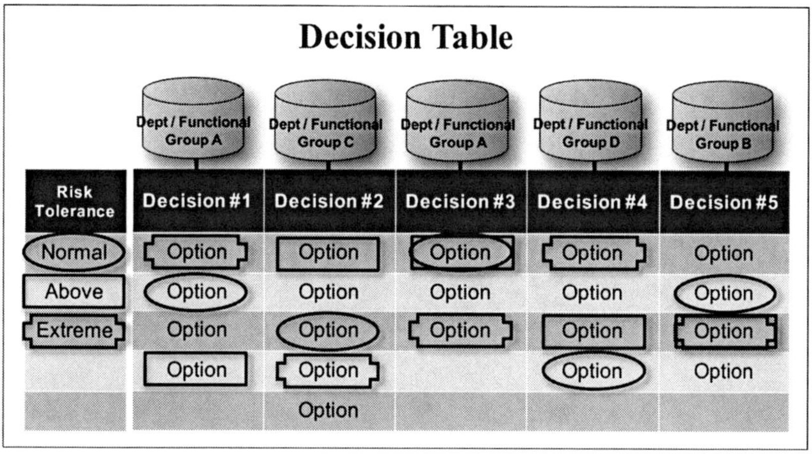

Figure 26

The additional Risk Tolerance sophistication requires more work:

- **One,** each Risk Tolerance Profile needs to be defined. For example, define what is meant by "Normal," "Above," and "Extreme." It is assumed the team is taking more risk to obtain higher rewards.

- **Two,** identify all risks associated with the work effort.

- **Three,** add Decisions and Decision Options to the Decision Table that would minimize risks (also known as "Risk Mitigation").

- **Four,** choose the appropriate decisions for each Risk Tolerance Profile.

- **Five,** for each Risk Tolerance Profile and associated decisions determine the overall Value. This is generally a ROI (Return on Investment) calculation. The work effort team and management collaborate to determine the best risk tolerance profile (path thru the Decision Table).

Exercise

Someone once said "An ounce of prevention is worth a pound of cure". As Mayor of a large City, a deadly flu has broken out. What are your Risk Mitigation decisions?

Loyal Subject can relate to considering different risks and associated decisions. At one time, Loyal was interested in raising cattle. Loyal had the opportunity to buy two cows. One cow was strong and healthy but, cost a lot of money. The other cow was quite a bit cheaper, it looked okay; but, had a slight limp. Needless to say, the Subject Family ate well that winter and Loyal never raised cattle.

Loyal goes back into future gaze....

Report Using Execution Plus®

An organizational work effort team presents information to management at a Management Decision Point. What's the best form or easiest way to document the information that is provided to management? Use Execution Plus®. Execution Plus® is a reporting format designed for use with the CSQ3® Optimum work flow system.

Use the Execution Plus® format at the end of the Concept, Structure, Detail, and Implement Phases. The format summarizes work performed by the work effort team; provides management with critical information for use at Management Decision Points; and, archives work effort information for future reference and evaluation.

A typical work effort is assumed to have a management team made up of a team leader with additional leaders from each significant functional area, and additional work effort team members assigned to their respective area of functional expertise.

The major areas of responsibility and activity related to the preparation of the Execution Plus® report can be simplified as follows:

Figure 27

Execution Plus® is divided into the following sections, with interlaced Cost, Schedule, and Quality information:

- **Introductory Section**
- **Summary Section**
- **Intermediate Sections (Repeated)**
- **Planning Section**

Work effort team management handles the Introductory, Summary and Planning Sections. These Sections are critical in Management Decision Point reviews and would also interest executive management. The Intermediate Sections are repeated for each significant functional area. Note: department management would certainly be interested in the work effort sections that pertain to their respective departments and functional areas.

The reporting format is as follows:

Execution Plus®

I. **Introductory Section**

   A. Organizational Work Effort Scope (answer the questions below)

      - What are we going to do?
      - Why are we doing it?
      - What does success look like?

   B. Current Phase

C. Identify Work Effort Team Members

- Reference an attachment of all team members (include team members from all previous Phases.)

D. Identify "Management Decision Point" Personnel

E. Include the most likely Cost, Schedule, and Value Estimates

- The estimates can be the average or "the most likely." The reported estimates will be utilized in future performance appraisals.
- With respect to Value Estimates, include ROI calculations.
- In the ROI calculations, clearly identify the investment.

F. Recommended Action

- "Kill" the work effort or "Approve" the continuation of the work effort to the next Phase.

II. **Summary Section**

A. Executive Summary and Highlights

- High level summary of the work effort with highlights written by work effort management.

B. Cost and Schedule Information

- Include appropriate work breakdown schedules with relevant costs.

C. Quality – "Value" Information

- Include financial assumptions and appropriate calculations.

D. Quality – "Decision Quality" Information

- Include work effort team management decisions from the Decision Table.

- Identify the department and functional group in the department that has responsible for each decision contained in the Decision Table.

E. Quality – "Risk Tolerance"

- Elaborate on the Risk Tolerance Profile(s) for making work effort decisions.

F. Quality – "Potential Risks and Risk Mitigation"

- Identify potential risks and risk mitigation plans.

G. Discussion/Conclusions

III. **Intermediate Sections (Repeat for Key Work Effort Groups or Functional Areas)**

A. Summary and Highlights for Each Key Group or Functional Area

B. Cost and Schedule Components

- Include the group's Cost and Schedule components.

C. Quality - Value Component

- Include the group's contribution to the Value component.

D. Quality – Decisions and Decision Options

- Include the group's section from the overall work efforts' Decision Table.

- Identify the department and functional group in the department that has responsible for each decision contained in the Decision Table.

E. Discussion/Conclusions

IV. **Planning Section**

- Identify the plans and requirements for the next phase. Provide next phase schedules, budgets, personnel and additional resource requirements, etc.

Use Execution Plus® as the official format for reporting work effort information. Estimates are important. Estimate ranges are: +/- 40% for the Concept Phase; +/- 25% for the Structure Phase; and +/- 15% for the Detail Phase. Note, in Execution Plus® Section I. E., report the average or most likely estimate. The reported information is critical to establishing work effort performance scores per CSQ3® Metrics.

Exercise

What are the positives for using a common reporting format, such as Execution Plus® at a Management Decision Point?

Loyal Subject likes the commonality of Execution Plus®. All key organizational work efforts would report information in a similar fashion. Personnel newly assigned to a work effort could easily skim through the reports from past phases or similar types of work efforts.

Loyal talked to the Supreme Ruler. "Simplify the management of the overall work flow system," "Provide key information with drill down capability" were the words from the Supreme Ruler.

Loyal Subject goes back into future gaze…

Emphasis Management Decision Points

In organizations the assignment of competent personnel to a Management Decision Point is especially critical. The future of the organization is dependent on their judgment.

The incorporation of Management Decision Points into work efforts has numerous benefits.

The Right Work is Being Done at the Right Time

First of all, the right work is being done at the right time. Besides being involved with the initial work effort scope, management is informed and agrees with the scope of work being performed in each phase. The objective of each phase is clear. The work effort team only performs work that is relevant to the current phase.

Management and the Work Effort Team Communicate

Second, the work effort team and management have a vested interest to communicate. The work effort team needs management's approval to move to the next phase. Management wants to keep informed about work effort activity, since management will have to make a decision at the end of their phase. If management is surprised at the results of a given phase, then, management and the work effort team are not communicating.

Management is Forced to Make a Decision

Third, management can only make a "Kill" or "Approve" decision. "Do the work phase over" or "Guess again at the answer" is not a management option. Hence, the "Never Ending" work effort is ended.

Note: it is better to Kill a bad work effort than to live with the results.

Manage the CSQ3® Optimum Three Level (Strategic, Major Commercial, and Project) System

CSQ3® Optimum is a three level organizational work flow system that is applicable to any organization. The three levels are Strategic, Major Commercial, and Project. Every CSQ3® Optimum work effort is placed in one and only one of the levels.

CSQ3® Optimum is based on the premise that strategy drives the capturing of major commercial opportunities which then drives the launching of projects.

CSQ3® Optimum

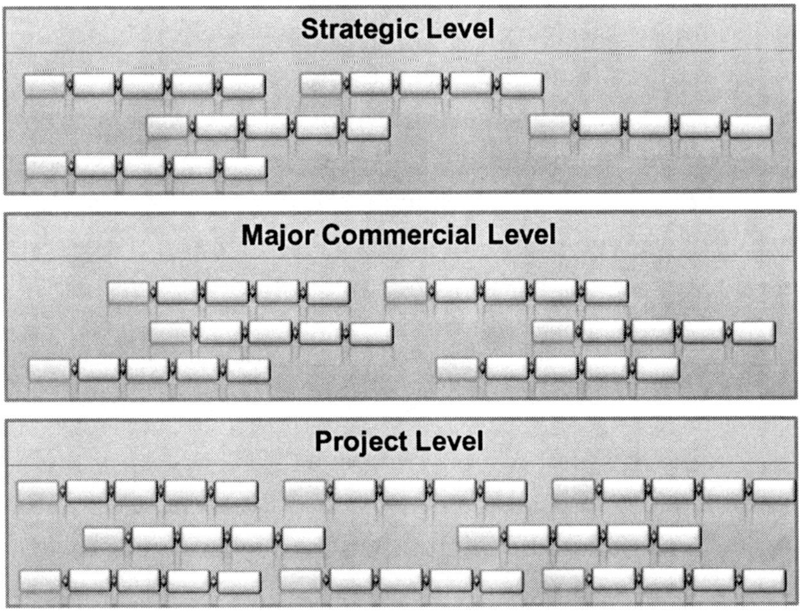

Figure 28

For example, assume that you are the new Chief Executive Officer of a technology organization, the organization has experienced no growth in the last few years and the organization's products are maturing.

- **Launch Strategic Work Effort:** You understand that change is needed, so you launch a strategic work effort to establish a five year plan for the organization. The developed plan has the following main items:

    1. Your organization will buy company "X". Company "X" has a portfolio of new and exciting products but, the new products rely on the purchase of a secret key ingredient from company "Y".

    2. Your organization will obtain the exclusive purchasing rights from company "Y".

    3. Your organization will build manufacturing plants throughout the world that will produce the new products.

- **Dependent Strategic Work Effort:** Buy company "X".

- **Dependent Major Commercial Work Effort:** Obtain the exclusive purchasing rights to the secret key ingredient from company "Y".

- **Dependent Project Work Efforts:** Depending on the success of the above work efforts, build manufacturing plants throughout the world.

Why Major Commercial? Does the Three Level System Change Over Time?

Strategy driving the capturing of major commercial deals and the launching of projects makes sense. All organizations make commercial deals. "Why is the middle level **Major Commercial**, as opposed to just **Commercial**?"

Executive management is absolutely interested in major commercial deals that impact the organization. A CSQ3® Optimum commercial work effort is considered major, if the work effort has a significant effect on an organization's bottom line and/or significant Project Level work efforts are then launched. Signing the exclusive purchasing deal for the secret ingredient allowed the launching of the manufacturing plant work efforts with potential large revenue streams.

Does the CSQ3® Optimum work flow structure change as an organization grows?

Organizations change over time. If successful, organizations go through a start-up period, a growth period, and then a mature period in their overall life cycle. For example, a major commercial deal (work effort) when an organization is getting started would probably be insignificant to the same organization when the organization is mature. Hence, work efforts that are placed in the Major Commercial Level have to be "Major/Significant" relative to the size and importance to the organization. Consequently, the three level structure of the CSQ3® Optimum work flow system does not change over time. The work efforts in the various levels change but, the three level structure remains constant.

Zoom...Zoom...Zoom

The degree of automation when implementing the CSQ3® Optimum work flow system is up to the respective organization. In some organizations the work flow system may be contained in a spreadsheet. In other organizations the work flow system may consist of numerous databases with possible tie ins to other organizational systems.

Assuming a sophisticated implementation of the CSQ3® Optimum work flow system in a medium or large organization, management has the ability to look at the big picture or zoom down to any degree of detail that they desire. For example, management can look at all work efforts, and make predictions for the future state of the organization. Management can look at the work efforts associated with one of the CSQ3® Optimum levels (Strategic, Major Commercial, or Project). Management can focus on similar work efforts or the specifics of just one work effort. Management can zoom down to individual work effort phases, review decision tables, cross reference any information in the system, etc. There are numerous possible tie-ins and automation possibilities with the CSQ3® Optimum organizational work flow system.

Making Management Easier

Management of the organization has just become easier!! All of the key organizational work efforts are located in the CSQ3® Optimum work flow system. Executive and department management can look at the entire picture or zoom into the particulars of any one work effort. Departments can become true Centers of Knowledge. Work effort teams are empowered. Work effort teams and management are engaged.

So how do we know if CSQ3® Optimum is working properly in an organization? When people working in the trenches say "Our Organization is Performing, the Right Work, at the Right Time, with the Right People!!"

Exercise

In your organization, who or what group would control or govern the CSQ3 Optimum work flow system?

Loyal Subject is in shock... It's too easy... Supreme Ruler can now monitor all of the key work efforts in the Land of Near! In addition, Supreme Ruler with automation can do that "Zoom, Zoom, Zoom Thing" and look at any aspect of a work effort that strikes Supreme's fancy...

But, wait!!

The Land of Far

just declared War on the

Land of Near!!

Supreme Ruler wants to use

Your New Found Knowledge of

CSQ3® Optimum in the

Battle with Far!

CSQ3® Optimum Test

For questions 1 thru 5, determine the proper CSQ3® Optimum work flow level.

1. There has been thievery in the armory! The Land of Near's stock pile of swords is gone! Purchase 10,000 swords from the Land of Merchants, Immediately!!

    A. Strategic Level

    B. Major Commercial Level

    C. Project Level

2. Reopen the metal mine in order to get raw materials for armor and additional swords.

    A. Strategic Level

    B. Major Commercial Level

    C. Project Level

3. Build 3 new blacksmith shops.

    A. Strategic Level

    B. Major Commercial Level

    C. Project Level

4. Develop an overall battle plan.

   A. Strategic Level

   B. Major Commercial Level

   C. Project Level

5. Develop a surrender plan, in case the battle goes wrong.

   A. Strategic Level

   B. Major Commercial Level

   C. Project Level

6. Supreme Ruler needs you to launch a work effort to disrupt and spy on the Land of Far. Which of the following are measures of success for the work effort team?

   A. Report on enemy movements over 1,000 strong within the borders of Far.

   B. Develop a network of 50 insurgents that will disrupt supply lines in Far.

   C. Attend the Province of Pain's annual Carnival.

   D. Obtain an initial assessment of the Land of Far's battle strength within 15 days from the deployment of spies.

7. In the past, the Province of Intellectus always developed battle plans; the Province of Thunder housed the troops, and the Province of Pain controlled the supply lines. Who do you assign on the work effort to develop the battle plan?

   A. The Province of Intellectus

   B. The Provinces of Intellectus and Thunder

   C. The Provinces of Intellectus, Thunder, and Pain

   D. Loyal Subject and Good Friend

8. Building of the Blacksmiths shops is proceeding slowly. There is a shortage of stone. The Decision is Building Material. What are possible Decision Options?

   A. Do Nothing

   B. Use Wood (non-fire locations)

   C. Pay More for Stone

   D. Tear down Stone Houses

9. The Army of Far is nearing the Province of Thunder. A major battle will begin within a week. What decisions can the Supreme Ruler make to mitigate risks?

A. Send in Reinforcements

B. Build more Blacksmith shops

C. Evacuate non-essential citizens

D. Ready Medical Supplies

10. The Detail Phase estimates are in for the reopening of the metal mine. What will be reported?

A. +/- 15% Accuracy Range

B. +/- 40% Accuracy Range

C. +/- 25% Accuracy Range

D. Average or most likely

1) B; 2) C; 3) C; 4) A; 5) A; 6) A, B, D; 7) C; 8) A, B, C, D;
9) A, C, D; 10) A, D

There is Celebration!!

The Land of Near Defeated the Land of Far!

All of the Provinces in the Land of Near now understand the effectiveness of Loyal Subject's teachings. In fact, the Province of Thunder will honor Loyal Subject with a festival! Supreme Ruler is proud of Loyal. CSQ3® Optimum is implemented in the Land of Near. Loyal moves forward to Challenge #3

Challenge #3: Achieving Excellence in the "Land of Near" (Teaching CSQ3® Metrics)

The 3rd Challenge is to implement a performance system that is applicable across the Land of Near (an organization). The performance system is to measure the success of key work efforts and the ability of the Land of Near to continually improve over time.

Loyal Subject is perplexed. The Challenge is too difficult. However, the People of Near are counting on Loyal.

Loyal Subject goes back into future gaze....

The intent of CSQ3® Metrics is to establish a performance system where organizations can monitor their progress over time, and compare their own organizational score to the scores of other organizations.

CSQ3® Metrics, which is based on the utilization of CSQ3® Optimum, has a maximum score of 10,000 points. Six thousand points are dedicated to the Delivery of Value.

Four thousand points are dedicated to the Creation of a Self Correcting Organization.

As shown in the figure, an organization scoring 9,000 points or more is classified as achieving "Organizational Excellence."

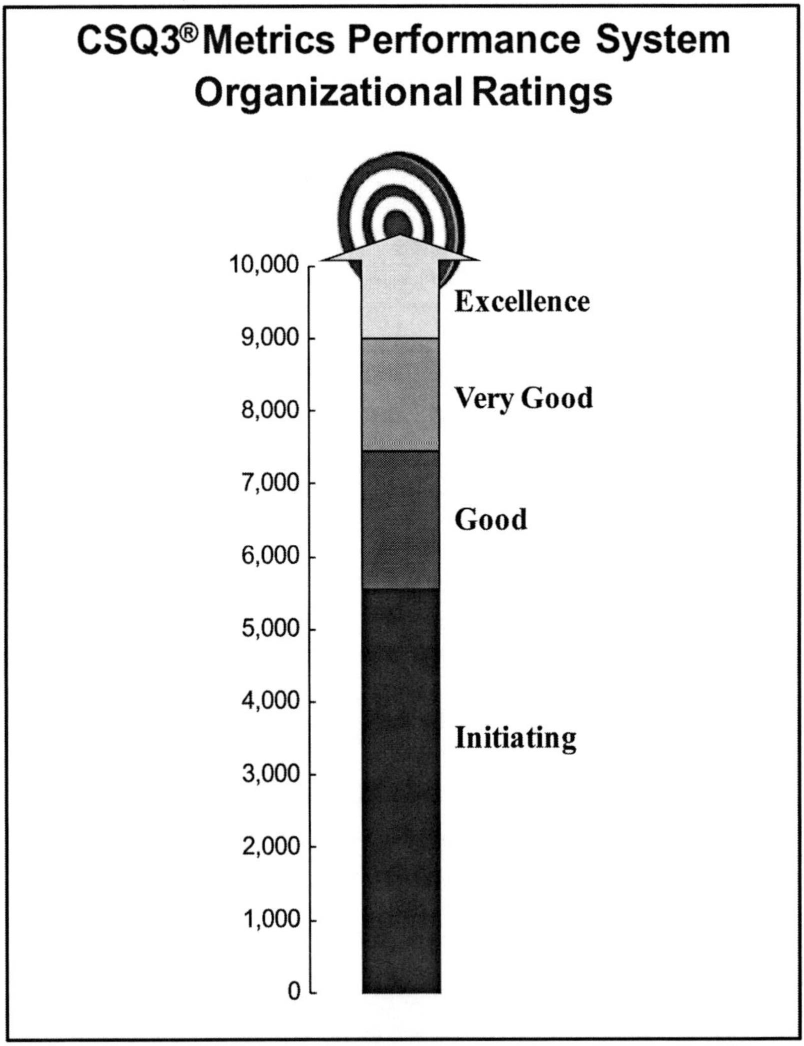

Figure 29

An organizational score of 7500 to 8999 is "Very Good." An organizational score of 5500 to 7499 is "Good." An organizational score below 5500 is considered an initiating period.

Delivering Value

Delivering Value is the focus of every CSQ3® Optimum work effort. Every work effort is broken into phases. Value estimates are made in the Concept, Structure, and Detail Phases; when a work effort reaches the Operate Phase "Actual Value" can be established.

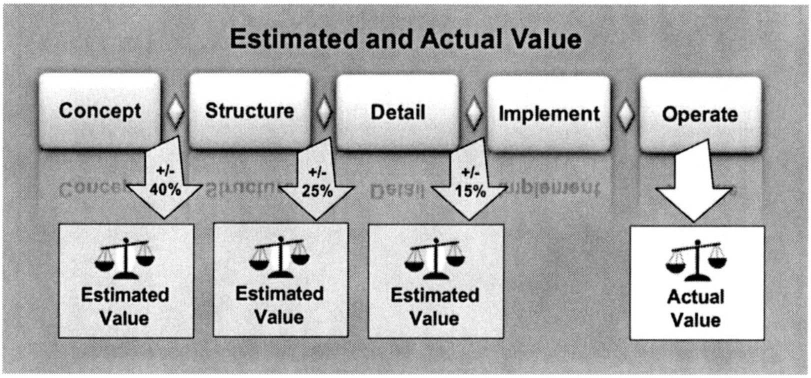

Figure 30

The CSQ3® Metrics "Delivering Value" score is based on the statement:

"Tell me What you are Going to Do, and Let's See if you Do It."

For every CSQ3® Optimum work effort that reaches the Operate Phase; "Estimated Value" is compared to "Actual Delivered Value." CSQ3® Metrics performance scores are then calculated for the work effort. The maximum score for any one work effort is 2,000 points.

There are however, numerous work efforts in every CSQ3® Optimum level. The maximum score for any level, Strategic, Major Commercial, or Project is 2,000 points. Level scores are prorated based on the total number of eligible work efforts in a level. The maximum CSQ3® Metrics "Delivering Value" score is 6,000 points.

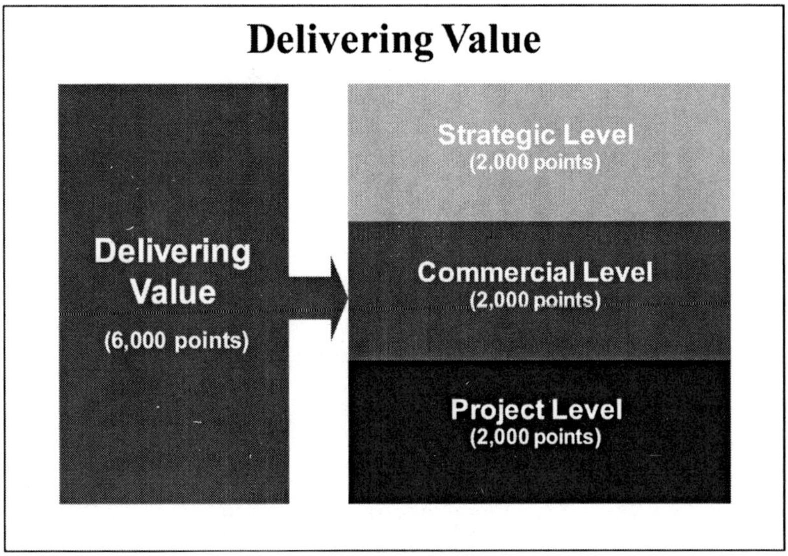

Figure 31

Loyal Subject understands the reasons for estimating Value and then comparing the estimates to Actual Value.

Loyal's friend, Good Friend, was running The Tavern when a shady looking torch seller came in, and wanted to sell Good Friend some torches. The prices were too low. Good Friend looked closely at the torches, and concluded that the torches would leak oil and possibly start a fire.

Good Friend realized that there was "No Value;" however, Good Friend sent the shady seller over to "Cheap Tavern" a competitor of The Tavern. And, now the competition is no more…

Loyal talks to Supreme Ruler. Scoring points for a work effort makes sense. Rolling up work effort scores in order to get a score for the entire Level seems okay but, why does Strategic, Major Commercial, and Project Levels have equal maximum scores of 2,000 points each? Isn't the Strategic Level more important? Why does Major Commercial rank so high?

All Levels are important. Strategy gives the direction but, signing major contracts and building new facilities are just as important. Remember in the battle with the Land of Far and the emergency purchase of 10,000 swords from the Land of Merchants. The Land of Near would have lost the battle if the swords weren't delivered in time. In fact, with the reopening of the mine and new blacksmith shops, the Land of Near will be offering the Land of Merchants a major new deal for the supply of armor. A work effort team is already in the Structure Phase. If successful, 10 additional blacksmith shops will be built in the Land of Near and the mine capacity will be expanded.

Loyal Subject is content. Loyal goes back to future gaze…

Creating a Self Correcting Organization

Another component of CSQ3® Metrics is the creation of a Self Correcting organization. Let's be realistic, in most organizations good news is highlighted and bad news is

Creating a Self Correcting Organization (4,000 points)

buried. How can an organization improve, if balanced feedback is not provided? So, how is a Self Correcting organization created?

• **First:** Everyone in the organization needs to speak the same language. In the land of CSQ3®, that includes: Work Efforts, Phases, Management Decision Points, Decision Tables, etc. The various work efforts will be different; but, everyone will understand the objectives and methodology for making work flow.

- **Second:** Work effort team members need honest feedback. Feedback on "Killed" work efforts and on work efforts that reach the Operate Phase need to be played back to all contributing work effort team members.

- **Third:** Organizational departments need honest feedback. Departments are "Centers of Knowledge" in the organization. Departments train personnel that are assigned to empowered work effort teams. Do the decisions, estimates, work activities, etcetera of the work effort team members adequately reflect the excellence of their home departments? Honest departmental and overall organizational feedback is critical to a "Self-Correcting" organization.

CSQ3® Metrics assigns 4,000 points to "Creating a Self-Correcting Organization." Two thousand (2000) points are allocated to the training, utilization, and capture of CSQ3® work effort methodology. One thousand (1000) points are allocated to improving work efforts, and one thousand (1000) points are allocated to improving departments.

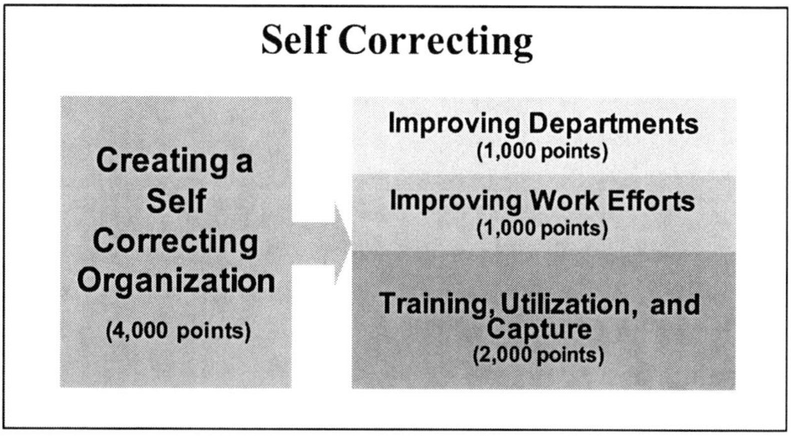

Figure 32

What would have to change in your organization in order to get honest (positive and negative) feedback to work effort teams and departments?

Loyal has to think about the possibility of creating a Self Correcting Organization. Loyal understands from the work with the populous of Near the power of getting everyone to speak the same language and the power of performing the right work, at the right time, with the right people. Honest feedback to work effort teams is probably doable but, honest feedback in the Province of Thunder seems like a life limiting endeavor.

In order to learn more, Loyal Subject goes back to future gaze...

Fundamental Appraisals

A Fundamental Appraisal is performed on every CSQ3® Optimum work effort. A Fundamental Appraisal is performed when a work effort is "Killed" or when a work effort reaches the Operate phase.

- Conduct a Fundamental Appraisal for every "Killed" organizational work effort. A work effort can be "Killed" at the end of Concept, Structure, and Detail Phases (and in rare occasions at the end of the Implement Phase).
- For work efforts that reach the Operate Phase, conduct a Fundamental Appraisal as soon as practical after the Operate Phase punch list items are worked out.

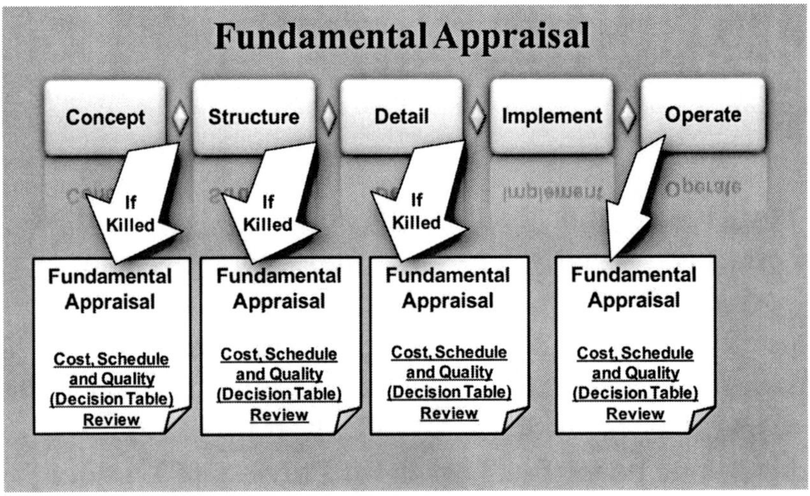

Figure 33

The Fundamental Appraisal reviews Cost, Schedule, and Decisions. The appraisal should provide meaning feedback to the work effort team, management, and other organizational entities. Cost and Schedule comparisons (actual versus estimate) per phase are appropriate. A close look at specific decisions and possible decision options is also appropriate. A review of risk assumptions, mitigations, and a reflection of risks on estimates is expected.

The Fundamental Appraisal should provide a holistic view of the key organizational work effort. What could we have done better? What did we do well? In which phase did we take a wrong turn? What could we have done different?

Every work effort entered into the CSQ3® Optimum work flow system should have a CSQ3® Metrics Fundamental Appraisal performed.

Exercise

Assume that you are responsible for conducting a Fundamental Appraisal. What would you include in the appraisal?

Loyal likes the idea of Fundamental Appraisals. Learning from past work efforts would be beneficial to new work effort teams. Comparing the Costs and Schedules of similar work efforts would make numbers people happy. Reviewing work effort decisions, what went right, what went wrong would be extremely helpful to all concerned.

Loyal goes back to future gaze…

Ultimate Appraisals

Costs, Schedules, and Decisions are important but, organizations implement work efforts to create "Actual Value." Conduct a CSQ3® Ultimate Appraisal on all CSQ3® Optimum work efforts that reach the Operate phase.

The primary purpose of the Ultimate Appraisal is to establish the Actual Delivered Value of a work effort. The Actual Value is compared to the Estimated Value that a work effort team documents in the Concept, Structure, and Detail Phases. The ratios between Estimated Value and Actual Value are used to establish the CSQ3® Metrics score for the work effort. Actual Value is determined in the Operate Phase when the work effort's measures of success can be fully and fairly evaluated. The highest point scores are obtained when Estimated Values are equal to the Actual Delivered Value of a work effort.

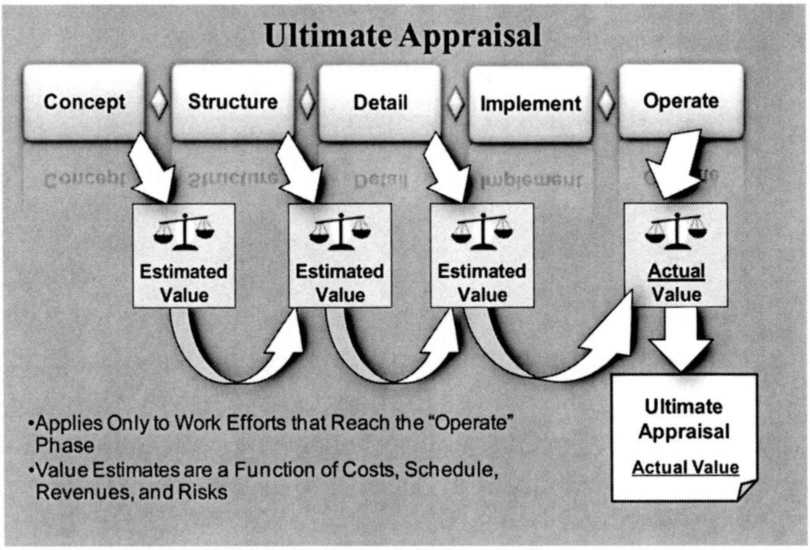

Figure 34

ROI is the Recommended Value Measure

Return on Investment (ROI) is the recommended financial measure for all CSQ3® Optimum work efforts. In its' simplest form, ROI = (Revenues – Investment) / Investment. Of course the time value of money, taxes, depreciation, etcetera should be included. In order to insure consistency, report Value in terms of ROI, and include relevant documentation.

Non-Profit ROI Example

What's the Return on Investment (ROI) for a non-profit organization? For example, a non-profit organization launches a work effort that will re-educate high school drop outs. The work effort will have space for 100 people per year with a total investment of $100,000 per year. Out of the 100 drop outs, 20 are expected to receive their high school diploma. The non-profit does not receive any revenue. However, assume society has a net benefit of $6,000 per year for each drop out that gets a diploma (higher wages, taxes, reduced medical costs, etcetera). Consequently the Revenue (Net Benefit) estimate is 20 x $6,000 = $120,000 per year. A simplified ROI = ($120,000 - $100,000) / $100,000 = 0.20 = 20%. When the work effort reaches the Operate Phase, the number of drop-outs actually getting a diploma can be determined and "Actual Value" assigned. The non-profit organization should be consistent in the assumptions and assignment of Value to its various work efforts. In all cases Actual Value needs to be correlated with measurable and tangible results.

Most Likely or Average Value Estimate Used in Scoring

Note, in the Concept, Structure, and Detail Phase the range in Estimated Value is +/-40%, +/-25%, and +/-15%, respectively. The "Reported Estimated Value" documented by the work effort team can be the "average of the range" or the "most likely." For example, a CSQ3® Optimum work effort is in the Concept Phase. The financial experts on the work effort team indicate that the average Return on Investment" (ROI) is 20%. The work effort can document 20% as their Estimated Value. The range in the ROI calculation is +/- 40% (note: 40% of 20% = 8%). Hence, ROI can be from 12% to 28%. On reflection the work effort team believes that the "most likely" ROI is 18%. The organizational work effort team can document the "most likely" in this case, 18% (instead of 20%) for their Concept Phase "Estimated Value." As covered in a previous section, Execution Plus® is a convenient format to consistently document work effort results.

Exercise

Ultimate Appraisals establish "Actual Delivered Value". At what point in the Operate Phase can "Actual Delivered Value" be determined? Use a past organizational work effort as an example.

Loyal Subject is about to call Good Friend since all these numbers are giving Loyal a headache. However, key work effort calculations are based on only four numbers: the reported Value estimate (average or most likely) in the Concept, Structure, and Detail Phases and the Actual

Value determined in the Operate Phase by an Ultimate Appraisal.

Loyal goes back to future gaze...

CSQ3® Point Scores

Every CSQ3® Optimum work effort can achieve a maximum of 2,000 points. In the ideal situation "Estimated Value" divided by "Actual Value" should equal one. Estimated Values are created in the Concept, Structure, and Detail Phases. The Actual Value is determined by an Ultimate Appraisal in the Operate Phase.

Points are awarded for the first three Phases as follows:

- Concept Phase 400 points (max)
- Structure Phase 600 points (max)
- Detail Phase 1,000 points (max)

The CSQ3® Point Scores Table provides the complete range of awarded points for various Value ratios. Once Actual Value is determined from an Ultimate Appraisal, the awarded score for the work effort can be determined. For the Concept, Structure, and Detail Phase, simply divide the respective estimated or most likely reported Value by the Actual Value determined in the Operate Phase. Use the calculated ratios to obtain the work effort's Concept Phase, Structure Phase, and Detail Phase score. Add up all three scores to get the total score for the work effort. The maximum score for any work effort is 2,000 points.

CSQ3® Point Scores Table

(Applies to Any CSQ3® Optimum Work Effort)

Ratio[1]	Concept Phase	Structure Phase	Detail Phase
Less than .549	240	360	600
.55 to .649	290	435	725
.65 to .749	330	495	825
.75 to .849	360	540	900
.85 to .949	380	570	950
.95 to 1.049	400	600	1000
1.05 to 1.149	380	570	950
1.15 to 1.249	360	540	900
1.25 to 1.349	330	496	825
1.35 to 1.449	290	435	725
Greater than 1.45	240	360	600

[1] Ratio = (Estimate "Average" or "Most Likely") / Actual

Rev.0

Figure 35

As an example, the Ultimate Appraisal of a CSQ3® Optimum work effort has reported the following results:

- Actual Delivered Value (Operate Phase), Return on Investment (ROI) = 20%
- Concept Phase (previously reported), ROI = 15%

- Structure Phase (previously reported), ROI = 18%
- Detail Phase (previously reported), ROI = 21%

Calculate Estimated to Actual Ratios

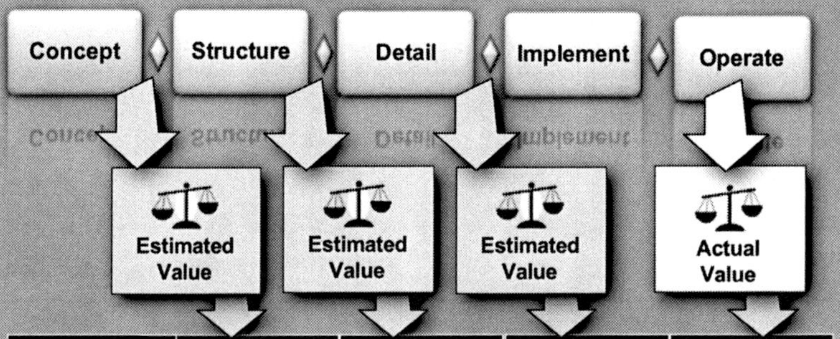

Item	Concept Phase	Structure Phase	Detail Phase	Operate Phase
Value Estimate	15	18	21	
Actual Value				20
Ratios	15/20= **.75**	18/20= **.90**	21/20= **1.05**	

Use Calculated Ratios to Determine Point Scores for the Work Effort

Figure 36

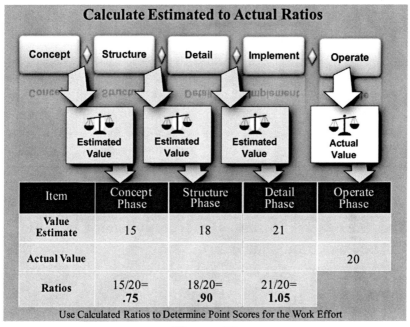

What are the CSQ3® Points awarded for the work effort?

- Concept Phase 15/20 = 0.75
    - Points per the table = **360**
- Structure Phase 18/20 = 0.90
    - Points per the table = **570**
- Detail Phase 21/20 = 1.05
    - Points per the table = **950**
- Total = 360 + 570 + 950 = <u>1,880 CSQ3® Points</u>

Ratio[1]	Concept Phase	Structure Phase	Detail Phase
Less than .549	240	360	600
.55 to .649	290	435	725
.65 to .749	330	495	825
.75 to .849	**360**	540	900
.85 to .949	380	**570**	950
.95 to 1.049	400	600	1000
1.05 to 1.149	380	570	**950**
1.15 to 1.249	360	540	900
1.25 to 1.349	330	496	825
1.35 to 1.449	290	435	725
Greater than 1.45	240	360	600
		Total Points	**1880**

[1] Ratio = Estimate Average/Actual

Figure 37

The above figure illustrates the scores obtained from the CSQ3® Point Scores Table.

Exercise

High work effort scores are achievable when Estimated Values are close to or equal to Actual Delivered Value. Why is this so?

Loyal Subject calls Good Friend. Loyal's hands are shaking, too many numbers, too many numbers! Good Friend takes Loyal to The Tavern.

Supreme Ruler visits Loyal Subject. Supreme Ruler did not know that dancing on top of a bar was appropriate behavior. Supreme Ruler gives Loyal a new abacus for number crunching. Loyal settles down and goes back to future gaze...

Roll Up Work Effort Scores to Strategic, Major Commercial, and Project Level Scores

There are three CSQ3® Optimum Levels: Strategic, Major Commercial, and Project. What is the maximum CSQ3® Metrics score per Level and how is the score calculated? The maximum score per Level is 2,000 points. The points per Level are rolled up based on the individual work effort point scores and actual investment.

For example, consider the Major Commercial Level of an organization that has four organizational work efforts that have reached the Operate Phase. Ultimate Appraisals were performed and points were awarded to each work effort. The awarded CSQ3® Points with associated investment for each work effort is as follows:

Major Commercial Work Effort	Total Work Effort Score		Investment ($ million)		Weighted Score
Work Effort 1	1,880	x	10	=	18,800
Work Effort 2	1,700	x	10	=	17,000
Work Effort 3	2,000	x	5	=	10,000
Work Effort 4	1,950	x	60	=	117,000
	Total		**85**		**162,800**
	Commercial Level Score (162,800/85)				**1,915**

Figure 38

Prorate work effort scores based on the actual work effort investment. Just multiply awarded work effort points times its investment (i.e. 1,880 x 10 = 18,800). Sum up the total (162,800). Divide the sum total, by the sum of all investments (162,800/85 = 1,915) to obtain the score for the Level.

Information Flow

The figure summarizes the flow of information in the calculation of Level Scores. An Ultimate Appraisal calculates a work effort score using archived Value estimates, Actual Value based on Operate Phase results, and the CSQ3® Point Score Table. Work effort scores are then prorated based on investment in order to obtain the score per Level.

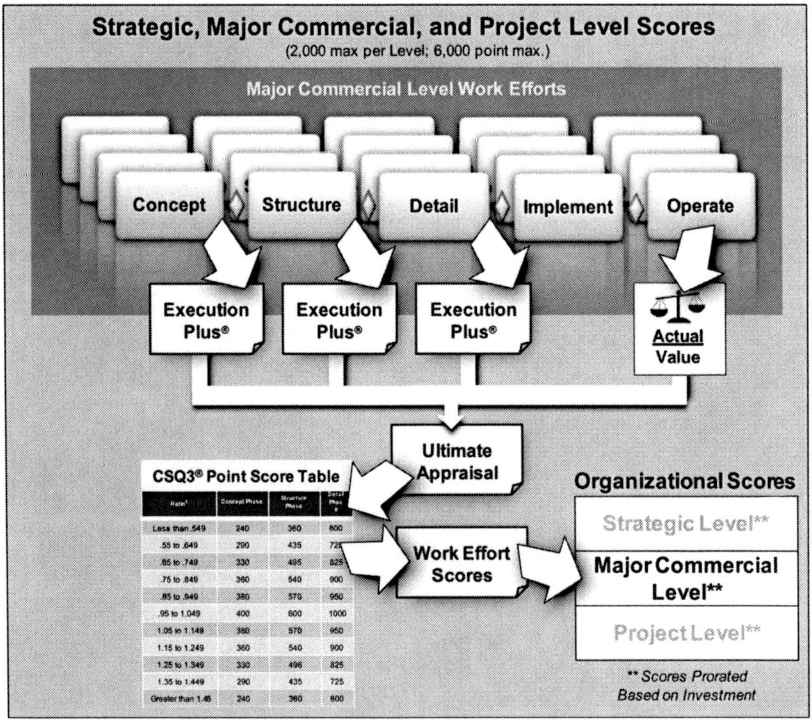

Figure 39

Assume similar calculations have been performed for the Strategic and Project Levels, with the following results:

Strategic Level	1,930 Points
Major Commercial Level	1,915 Points
Project Level	1,850 Points
Total (Delivering Value) Score	5,695 Points

Figure 40

Loyal Subject likes the new abacus from the Supreme Ruler. Calculations are a lot easier. In fact, Loyal is starting to comprehend all this number stuff.

Supreme Ruler checks on Loyal from a distance.

Loyal Subject goes back to future gaze…

Creating a Self Correcting Organization - Calculations

Creating a self correcting organization takes time. Active governance of the CSQ3® Optimum organizational workflow system and the CSQ3® Metrics organizational performance scoring system is required. The scores associated with the creation of a self correcting organization are for the most part a check that the work on the systems is being performed. Assuring that the work is being performed to the highest standards and is meaningful, is management's responsibility.

The 4000 point maximum Self Correcting component of the CSQ3® Metrics scoring system has three main sections:

- **Training, Utilization, and Capture (2,000 points max)**
- **Improving Work Efforts (1,000 points max)**
- **Improving Departments* (1,000 points max)** (*Can also include higher segments of the organization, i.e. divisions, sectors, etc.)

Training, Utilization, and Capture (2,000 point max)

Training has a maximum score of 1000 points, Utilization 500 points, and Capture 500 points. Details are as follows:

Training of Personnel in the Organization (1,000 points max) is calculated per the following formula:

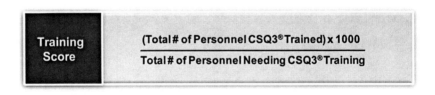

$$\text{Training Score} = \frac{(\text{Total \# of Personnel CSQ3}^{\circledR}\text{ Trained}) \times 1000}{\text{Total \# of Personnel Needing CSQ3}^{\circledR}\text{ Training}}$$

- Total number of personnel CSQ3® trained
    - The organization needs to determine the type of training and any certification requirements.

- Total number of personnel needing CSQ3® training
    - The organization needs to determine how many people will be trained.
    - An overview of CSQ3® methodology is recommended for all personnel in the organization.

Utilization of CSQ3® Methodology (500 points max) is calculated per the following formula:

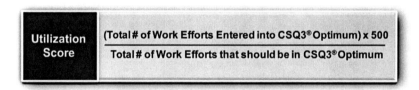

$$\text{Utilization Score} = \frac{(\text{Total \# of Work Efforts Entered into CSQ3® Optimum}) \times 500}{\text{Total \# of Work Efforts that should be in CSQ3® Optimum}}$$

- Total number of work efforts entered into CSQ3® Optimum
    - This is the current number of work efforts in the CSQ3® Optimum work effort system.
- Total number of work efforts that should be in CSQ3® Optimum
    - Management should review high cost single department work efforts (which in numerous cases should be multi-department) for inclusion in the CSQ3® Optimum workflow system.
    - When initiating CSQ3® Optimum in an organization there will be a difference between the number of work efforts in the system and

the number of work efforts that should be in the system.

- During initiation, there will be on-going key organizational work efforts that are not using CSQ3® methodology. Include the on-going work efforts in the above total.

Capturing Data (500 points max) is calculated per the following formula:

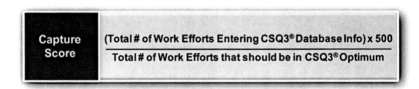

$$\text{Capture Score} = \frac{(\text{Total \# of Work Efforts Entering CSQ3® Database Info}) \times 500}{\text{Total \# of Work Efforts that should be in CSQ3® Optimum}}$$

- Total number of work efforts entering CSQ3® information into a central depository (a database is assumed)
    - Every organization needs to establish the degree of sophistication with respect to creating and accessing work effort information and knowledge.
    - Work effort teams need to enter their information into a central depository, use of Execution Plus® is recommended.
    - The central depository (database) information will be utilized to improve work efforts and departments.

- Total number of work efforts that should be in CSQ3® Optimum
    - See comments in the "Utilization Score" description.

Improving Work Efforts (1,000 points max)

Improving work efforts has a maximum score of 1000 points. Five hundred (500) points are associated with conducting CSQ3® Fundamental Appraisals. Two hundred fifty (250) points are associated with issuing Fundamental Appraisal reports. Two hundred fifty (250) points are associated with conducting Ultimate Appraisals.

Conducting CSQ3® Fundamental Appraisals (500 points max) is calculated per the following formula:

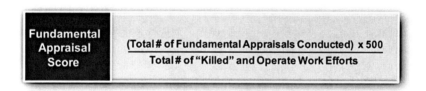

$$\text{Fundamental Appraisal Score} = \frac{(\text{Total \# of Fundamental Appraisals Conducted}) \times 500}{\text{Total \# of "Killed" and Operate Work Efforts}}$$

- Total number of Fundamental Appraisals conducted
    - The total number is a cumulative count of the conducted Fundamental Appraisals.
- Total number of Killed and Operate Phase work efforts

- A Fundamental Appraisal should occur whenever a work effort is Killed or when the work effort enters the Operate Phase.

Issuing Fundamental Appraisal reports to all Work Effort Team Members (250 points max) is calculated per the following formula:

$$\text{Team Distribution Score} = \frac{(\text{Total \# of Fundamental Appraisals Conducted and Sent to All Team Members}) \times 250}{\text{Total \# of Fundamental Appraisals Conducted}}$$

- Total number of Fundamental Appraisals conducted and sent to all team members
    - A Fundamental Appraisal performed on a Killed or Operate Phase work effort, needs to be sent to all team members associated with any phase of the work effort.
    - It is imperative to track all team members and significant contributors associated with any phase of a work effort.
    - Sending Fundamental Appraisals to significant work effort contributors is recommended but, it is not a requirement.
    - It is common for some personnel that get involved with the early phases of a work effort to be reassigned before the work effort reaches the Implement and Operate Phases.

If personnel do not know what the mistakes are, they cannot learn from their mistakes. In addition, things that are working extremely well or provided for a competitive or customer advantage should be repeated.

- The Total number of Fundamental Appraisals conducted
    - A Fundamental Appraisal should occur whenever a work effort is Killed or when the work effort enters the Operate Phase.

Conducting CSQ3® Ultimate Appraisals (250 points max) is calculated per the following formula:

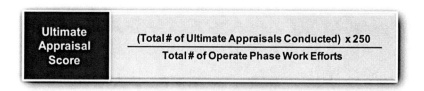

$$\text{Ultimate Appraisal Score} = \frac{(\text{Total \# of Ultimate Appraisals Conducted}) \times 250}{\text{Total \# of Operate Phase Work Efforts}}$$

- Total number of Ultimate Appraisals conducted
    - The total number of Ultimate Appraisals is a cumulative value.
    - Conduct an Ultimate Appraisal as soon as "Actual Value" can be determined in the Operate Phase.
    - Ultimate Appraisals establish the point awards for individual CSQ3® Optimum work efforts.

- Total number of Operate Phase work efforts
    - The total number of work efforts that reach the Operate Phase is a cumulative value.
    - Note there will be a time lag from when a work effort enters the Operate Phase and when the "Actual Value" can be determined in the Operate Phase.

Improving Departments* (1,000 points max)

(Can also include higher segments of the organization, i.e. divisions, sectors, etc.)*

Improving departments has a maximum score of 1000 points. Two hundred fifty (250) are associated with correlating work effort information with referenced departments. Two hundred fifty (250) points are associated with evaluating departments. Five hundred (500) points are associated with sending improvement reports to departments. Note, for simplicity it is assumed that an organization is made up of departments. An organization can also have divisions, sectors, etc. Treat the divisions and sectors as additional entities that require improvement reports.

Obtain information including Fundamental and Ultimate Appraisals on a representative sample of CSQ3® Optimum work efforts. Separate the information by departments and if possible by functional groups within departments. Calculate the score per the following formula (250 points max):

$$\text{Department Information Score} = \frac{(\text{Total \# of Departments With Actual Work Effort Info}) \times 250}{\text{Total \# of Departments in the Organization}}$$

- Total number of departments with actual work effort information
    - The purpose is to collect enough representative work effort data to draw conclusions on the performance of departments.
    - Information is obtainable from Decision Tables and estimates of Cost, Schedule, and Value.?
    - Include divisions and sectors etcetera if appropriate.
- Total number of departments in the organization
    - Departments are Centers of Knowledge in the organization. Include all departments in the total.
    - Include divisions and sectors etcetera if appropriate.

Analyze work effort information in order to establish the Strengths and Weaknesses of Departments. Calculate the score per the following formula (250 points max):

$$\text{Department Evaluation Score} = \frac{(\text{Total \# of Departments With Strengths \& Weaknesses Established}) \times 250}{\text{Total \# of Departments in the Organization}}$$

- Total number of departments with strengths and weaknesses established
    - The organization needs to establish the format for the strengths and weaknesses analysis. The analysis should be meaningful and relevant.
- Total number of departments in the organization
    - Departments are Centers of Knowledge in the organization. Include all departments in the total.
    - Include divisions and sectors etc.

Recommend Performance Improvement action to individual departments. Calculate the score per the following formula (500 points max):

$$\text{Department Action Score} = \frac{(\text{Total \# of Departments Receiving Improvement Action Reports}) \times 500}{\text{Total \# of Departments in the Organization}}$$

- Total number of departments receiving improvement action reports

- o The organization needs to establish the format and time frame between departmental improvement reports. Out dated or meaningless reports will not improve the organization.

- Total number of departments in the organization
  - o Include all departments in the total.
  - o Include divisions and sectors etc.

Organizational Governance

In addition to the conducting of Fundamental and Ultimate Appraisals, organizational governance of the entire CSQ3® Metrics performance scoring system is extremely important. CSQ3® Metrics establishes the framework for measuring organizational performance.

The degree of automation and detailed reporting mechanisms are left up to each organization in their governance procedures. Management in each organization is responsible for making the detailed reports meaningful, reasonable, and useful.

Without going through all the detailed calculations, what would a summary report look like for the "Creating a Self Correcting Organization" component of the CSQ3® Metrics performance scoring system?

Example Summary Report

Creating a Self Correcting Organization

Training, Utilization & Capture	
Training	900 Points
Utilization	450 Points
Capturing Data	480 Points
Improving Work Efforts	
Conducting Fundamental Appraisals	420Points
Issuing Reports	220 Points
Conducting Ultimate Appraisals	230 Points
Improving Departments	
Obtaining Information	240 Points
Analyzing Information	180 Points
Recommending Improvement	350 Points
Total (Self Correcting) Score	**3,470 Points**

Figure 41

Exercise

Point awards for the "Self-Correcting" component of CSQ3® Metrics is dependent on the organization making the information meaningful. Is your organization ready for the cultural shift?

Loyal Subject takes in all in. The calculations are pretty easy. Getting all of the information will take some work.

Loyal Subject talks to Supreme Ruler and Loyal receives all of the necessary resources to implement CSQ3® Metrics, Challenge #3 in the Land of Near.

Achieving Organizational Excellence

Delivering Value
(6,000 points)

Recapping, in order to determine organizational performance, Fundamental and Ultimate Appraisals are performed. A Fundamental Appraisal is performed when a work effort is "Killed," or when a work effort enters the Operate phase. The purpose of the Fundamental Appraisal is to examine the Cost, Schedule, and Decisions made by a work effort team. An Ultimate Appraisal is performed when a work effort reaches the Operate Phase and "Actual Value" can be determined. The purpose of the Ultimate Appraisal is to compare Estimated Value to Actual Value, and to establish the

CSQ3® Metrics score for the CSQ3® Optimum entered work effort. There are numerous work efforts per each CSQ3® Level. Individual work effort scores are prorated based on investment in order to establish CSQ3® Strategic Level, Major Commercial Level, and Project Level scores. There is a maximum of 2,000 points per Level or 6,000 Delivering Value points possible in total.

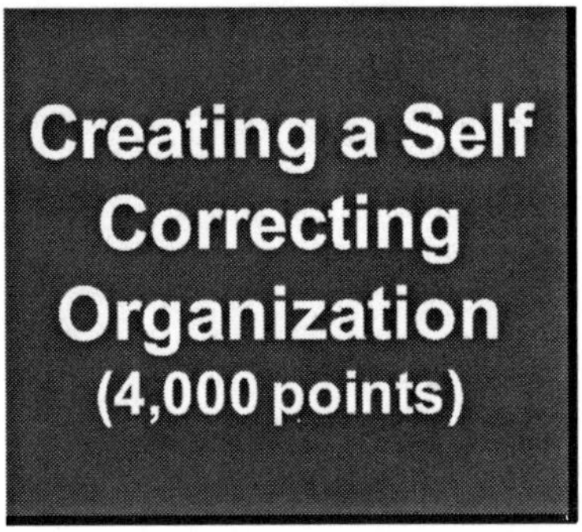

The self correcting component of CSQ3® Metrics is broken into three areas: Training, Utilization, and Capture; Improving Work Efforts; and, Improving Departments. Training, Utilization, and Capture has a maximum score of 2,000 points. Improving Work Efforts and Improving Departments, each have a maximum score of 1,000 points. The intent is to use Fundamental and Ultimate Appraisal information to provide honest feedback to work effort team members and all appropriate organizational entities. Improvement is founded in the knowledge of understanding what is working correctly, and what needs to be fixed.

Organizational Excellence Scores

So, "How many CSQ3® Metrics points are needed for an organization to claim "Excellence"?

CSQ3® Metrics defines "Organizational Excellence" as a score of 9,000 points or more. A score of 7,500 to 8,999 points is "Very Good." A score of 5,500 to 7,499 points is

"Good." A score of less than 5,500 points is considered an "Initiating" period.

Achieving "Organizational Excellence"

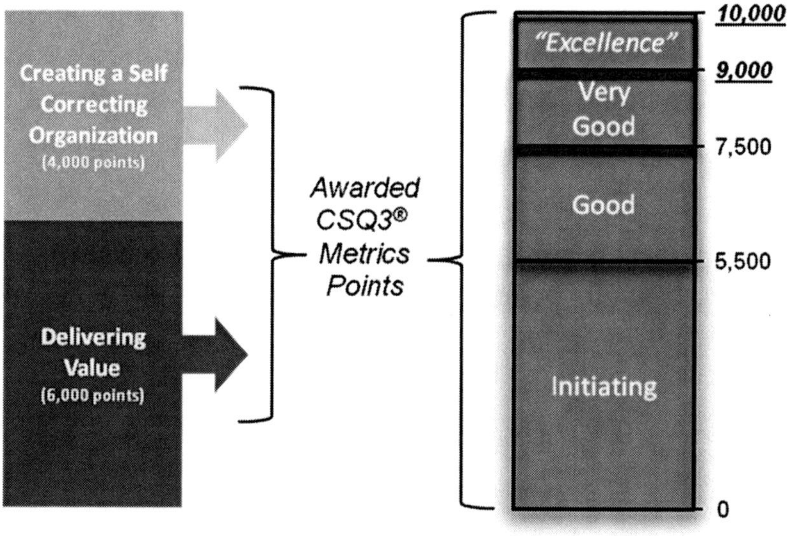

Figure 42

Achieving Excellence will take time. People need training. CSQ3® Optimum has to be populated with work efforts; CSQ3® Metrics needs data to develop scores, etc. Does your organization have the heart to embark on the adventure? The rewards are there, is your organization willing to take them?

Loyal Subject is in awe at the potential. Management can look at all of the key organizational work efforts in total, or drill down to any work effort detail. The need for management and work effort teams to interact is inherent in the CSQ3® methodology. Work effort teams are empowered but, can't get too carried away because of the Management Decision Points. Departments become Centers of Knowledge. "The organization performs the Right Work, at the Right Time, with the Right People." Personnel are focused on achieving Cost, Schedule, and Quality excellence.

Supreme Ruler congratulates Loyal Subject. The populous understands the power of CSQ3® Fundamentals. All of the Provinces in the Land of Near, and especially Intellectus, Thunder, and Pain have endorsed CSQ3® Optimum and CSQ3® Metrics.

Loyal Subject is guiding the Land of Near to Excellence. We owe it to our people...

Achieve Organizational Excellence !!!

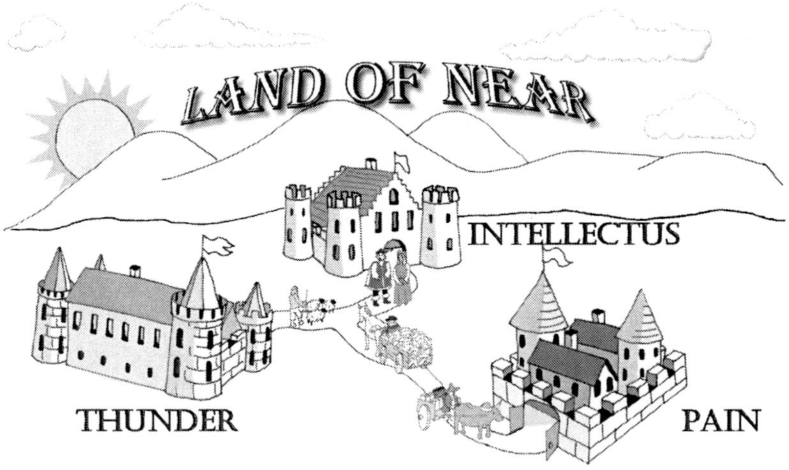

Figure 43

CSQ3® Metrics Test

1. What is "Zoom Zoom Zoom"?

    A. Loyal Subject's future gaze ability

    B. Ability to view organizational work in total (Strategic, Major Commercial, and Project Levels) and the ability to also view the specifics of any given work effort.

    C. Innate management ability

    D. New device to watch the Land of Far

2. What type of work efforts should be entered into CSQ3® Optimum?

    A. Department work efforts designated by management

    B. All work efforts that involve multiple departments

    C. Individual department renovations

    D. Individual work efforts

3. Who determines and scopes out all work efforts?

    A. Work effort teams

    B. Loyal Subject

    C. Supreme Ruler

D. Management

4. The CSQ3® Point Scores Table can be applied to which estimates?

    A. Cost

    B. Value

    C. Schedule

    D. Decision

5. The awarded CSQ3® Point Scores are based on what ratio?

    A. Estimated Cost / Actual Cost

    B. Estimated Value / Actual Value

    C. Estimated Schedule / Actual Schedule

    D. Estimated Revenue / Actual Revenue

6. Work effort scores are rolled up to Strategic, Major Commercial, or Project Level Scores. The work efforts are prorated based on what variable?

    A. Investment

    B. Revenue

    C. Costs

    D. Schedule

7. Fundamental Appraisals focus on the following:

    A. Cost

    B. Schedule

    C. Decisions

    D. Value

8. Ultimate Appraisals focus on the following:

    A. Cost

    B. Schedule

    C. Decisions

    D. Value

9. A Fundamental Appraisal is performed:

    A. At the end of every Phase

    B. At the beginning of the Operate Phase

    C. Whenever a work effort is Killed

    D. Before the Implement Phase

10. Achieving 'Excellence" requires how many points?

    A. 7,500 to 8,999

    B. 5,500 to 7,499

    C. 9,000 to 10,000

D. 5,000 Delivering Value Points

1) B; 2) A,B; 3) D; 4) A, B,C; 5) B; 6) A; 7) A, B, C;
8) D; 9) B, C; 10) C

Implementing the CSQ3® Solution in Your Organization

Implementing the CSQ3® Solution in your organization can be demanding. However, the potential rewards are significant. There will be political posturing and power plays. Individual departments will claim that they are already the best. They do not need to improve. However, the CSQ3® Solution is not about any one department, it's about establishing the best organizational solution to any given opportunity. Consistently achieving Cost, Schedule, and Quality excellence is possible. The potential gains from an economic viewpoint alone are overwhelming. Implement the CSQ3® Solution in your organization.

Fortunately, you already have the knowledge to implement CSQ3®. **CSQ3® implementation is a work effort.** CSQ3® is Cost, Schedule, and Quality raised to the 3rd Power. The 1st Power of the Solution is CSQ3® Fundamentals. Fundamentals establishes the basic methodology for implementing any work effort. The 2nd Power is CSQ3® Optimum, which builds on the methodology of CSQ3® Fundamentals to establish an organizational work flow system. The 3rd Power is CSQ3® Metrics, which utilizes the CSQ3® Optimum work flow system to establish an organizational performance scoring system. All three powers are described in this book. All upper management has to do is authorize their implementation.

To provide specific implementation guidance for every type of organization would be impossible to do, hence a higher level discussion is provided. The following figure highlights major management and organizational improvement team steps:

Improvement Effort – Implementing The CSQ3® Solution

Management

- Decides to Initiate an Organizational Improvement Effort
- Clearly Identifies the Improvement Effort Scope, Including Measurements of Success
- Forms the Organizational Improvement Work Effort Team

Organizational Improvement Team (Work Effort)

- Learns CSQ3® Methodologies and Systems
- Performs Work in CSQ3® Phases: Concept, Structure, Detail, Implement, and Operate
- In each Phase, Develops Decision Tables; and, Cost, Schedule, and Quality Information

Management

- Interacts with the Organizational Improvement Team, and Reviews All Phase Decisions and Recommendations. At every Management Decision Point the work effort is either "Killed" or "Approved to the Next Phase"

Figure 44

Work Effort Scope

A key management step is clearly identifying the scope of the improvement effort. In fact, the scope should be established before the formation of the improvement team. There are basically three questions that need to be answered in establishing the scope in any work effort: "What are we going to do?" "Why are we doing it?" and "What does success look like?"

The first two questions are easy to answer. Implement the CSQ3® Solution and improve the performance of the organization. However, the answer to the question "What does success look like?" needs careful consideration by management. Management needs to provide specific measures of success. A few suggestions are provided in the figure.

Improvement Effort Scope

What are We Going to Do?

- Implement an Organizational Improvement Effort Utilizing CSQ3® Methodologies and Systems

Why are We Doing It?

- Improve the Performance of the Organization

What Does Success Look Like?

- Management Needs to Provide Specifics, for example:
  - Train 80% of the Organization in CSQ3® Fundamentals within 3 months (time is measured from the start of the Implement Phase)
  - Implement the CSQ3® Optimum Work Flow System in 6 months
  - Establish a CSQ3® Metrics Utilization score of at least 450 points within 1 year

Figure 45

Improvement Team Formation

Team formation is very critical to the success of the effort. Team membership from all major departments in the flow of work activity is recommended. One of the goals of the CSQ3® Solution is to tear down department walls. If your critical departments are not involved in the development of the improvement effort, getting their buy-in at a later date will be difficult. Strategic, commercial, and project personnel and perspectives are vital to implementation success.

Once the work effort team is formed, they will need to learn and understand the CSQ3® Solution. Note: additional tools are available at the CSQ3® web site.

Work Effort Phases

Specific work activities in each work effort phase are dependent on the characteristics of each individual organization. However, major elements of work to be considered; and, the intent of each phase are highlighted in the accompanying sections.

Concept Phase

The Concept Phase is a look at the "Big Picture." Are there any "Show Stoppers" or "Opportunities" that we need to consider?

CSQ3® Optimum and CSQ3® Metrics are organizational systems. At least two "Big Picture" questions need resolution:

- Should the new systems be tied into any other organizational systems?
- What department (new or existing) will be responsible for the overall operation of the new systems?

Note: The systems include every key Strategic, Commercial, and Project work effort in the organization. Cost, Schedule, and Quality information will have to be obtained and maintained. Fundamental and Ultimate Appraisals performed. Feedback will need to be provided to work effort teams and departments.

Example Concept Phase decisions and considerations are provided in the figure.

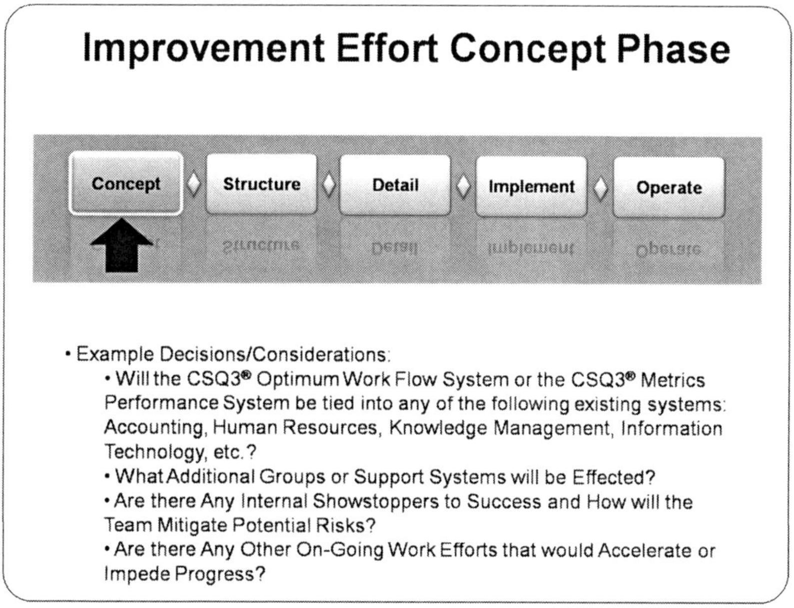

Figure 46

At the end of each phase, the organizational improvement team reports to management and, management decides if the work effort should continue. The work being performed is very significant. The work effort team is shaping the future and culture of the entire organization.

Structure Phase

The "Framework" of the implementation solution is established in the Structure phase. Major pieces of the framework are already laid out. Teach CSQ3® Fundamentals and establish CSQ3® Optimum and CSQ3® Metrics systems in your organization. Significant details and guidelines are provided. Structure phase activity includes implementation and interface decisions for your specific organization. Example Structure Phase decisions and considerations are provided in the figure.

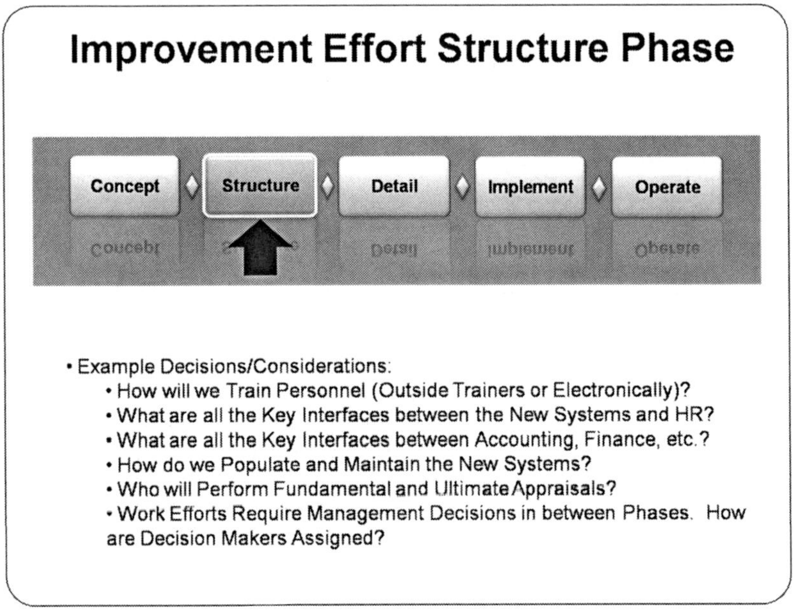

Figure 47

Detail Phase

The Detail phase puts the "Meat on the Bones." Fill in the framework details. The implementation plan is developed in three phases: Concept, Structure and Detail. At the end of the Detail phase, management should have all the details to substantiate +/- 15% estimates of Cost, Schedule, and Value. Management should be in agreement with the decisions established by the improvement effort team and documented in Decision Quality tables. At the end of the

Detail phase management should be able to give a thumbs up or down to the improvement effort. The work performed by the team should: "Clearly establish what you are going to do, before doing it." Example Detail phase decisions and considerations are highlighted.

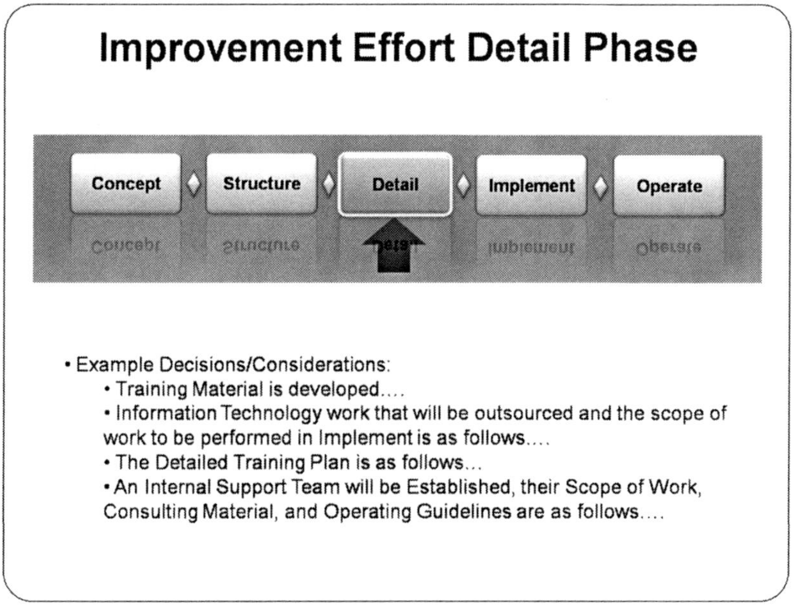

Figure 48

Implement Phase

The comprehensive improvement plan is developed, management decides to "Make It Happen" in the Implement phase. Sign appropriate contracts, build needed infrastructure, monitor contract activity, and start training personnel in the organization. Finalize the make-up of any operating or support team personnel. Train personnel and test for understanding.

Work with new work effort teams; establish the CSQ3® Optimum and CSQ3® Metrics systems. Work with management on internal marketing and support efforts, etc. Example Implement Phase decisions and considerations are provided in the figure.

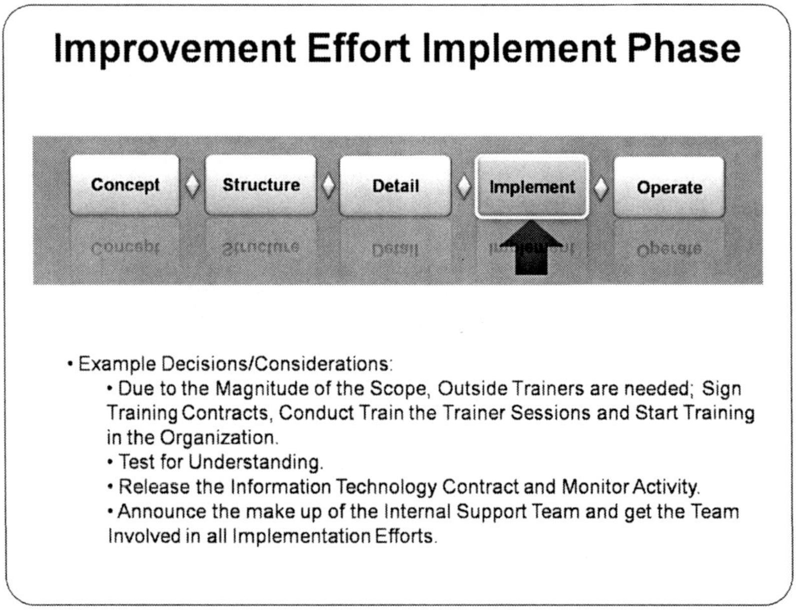

Improvement Effort Implement Phase
Concept
Structure
Detail
Implement
Operate
• Example Decisions/Considerations:
• Due to the Magnitude of the Scope, Outside Trainers are needed; Sign Training Contracts, Conduct Train the Trainer Sessions and Start Training in the Organization.
• Test for Understanding.
• Release the Information Technology Contract and Monitor Activity.
• Announce the make up of the Internal Support Team and get the Team Involved in all Implementation Efforts.

Figure 49

Operate Phase

Manage the CSQ3® Optimum and CSQ3® Metrics systems, and train additional personnel as needed in the Operate phase. Continue support to work effort teams. Conduct appropriate workshops. Perform Appraisals. Maintain Cost, Schedule, and Quality databases. Make sure that management and appropriate personnel can access work effort information. Develop management reports. Perform the work necessary to create a self correcting organization. Determine the CSQ3® Metrics performance score, etc. Example Operate Phase decisions and considerations are provided in the figure.

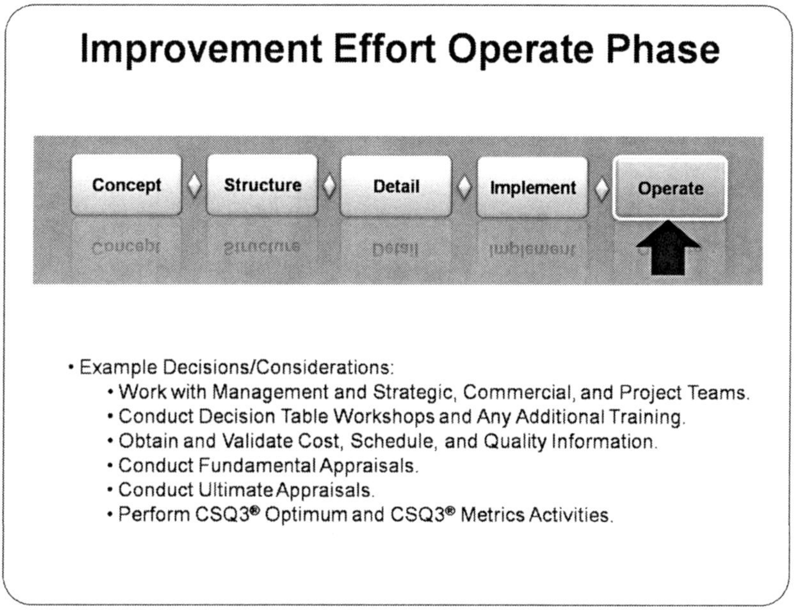

Figure 50

In Summary

In summary, the CSQ3® Solution can improve the performance and change the culture of your entire organization. Cost, Schedule, and Quality excellence is achievable. Organizational Excellence is achievable. Achieve Organizational Excellence!!!

For additional information, including courses, certification, and CSQ3® Consulting Group assistance visit the CSQ3® web site:

www.csq3.com

[1] The referenced Roundtable is actually "The Business Roundtable," which is an association of Chief Executive Officers committed to improving public policy. The referenced publication "The Business Stake in Effective Project Systems" was reprinted in September 1997.

[2] "Ideas to Reality" A High Level look at Business Processes that make Complex Business Systems work better for you the Shareholder, 2nd International Conference on the Dynamics of Strategy, Frank Koczwara, Jack Morbey, University of Surrey, U.K.

[3] See www.csq3.com web site

CSQ3® Content Summary

CSQ3® CONTENT SUMMARY	Fundamentals	Optimum	Metrics
Work Efforts	✓		
Key Organizational Work Efforts		✓	✓
Work Effort Components			
Phases	✓	✓	✓
Decision Points	✓	✓	✓
Cost Estimates	✓	✓	✓
Schedule Estimates	✓	✓	✓
Quality - Value Estimates	✓	✓	✓
Quality - Decision Tables	✓	✓	✓
Includes Key Work Efforts		✓	✓
Established Scope		✓	✓
Empowered Teams		✓	✓
Assigned Personnel/Resources		✓	✓
Tracked Responsibility		✓	✓
Execution Plus®		✓	✓
Management Decision Points		✓	✓
Governance – Three Level System		✓	✓
Delivering Value			✓
Determine Work Effort and Level Scores			✓
Fundamental Appraisals			✓
Ultimate Appraisals			✓
Creating a Self Correcting Organization			✓
Training, Utilization and Capture			✓
Improving Work Efforts			✓
Improving Departments			✓
Governance – Performance System			✓

Definitions

Centers of Knowledge – Departments are created in order to manage functional groups and train personnel. Departments are "Centers of Knowledge" for the contained functional areas.

Concept Phase – is the "Big Picture" division of any work effort. Cost, Schedule, and Value estimates are +/- 40%.

Cost Estimate – is the estimated monetary cost for a work effort to reach the Operate Phase. Cost estimates are provided at the end on the Concept, Structure, and Detail Phases with accuracies of +/- 40%, +/- 25%, and +/- 15%, respectively.

CSQ3® - is Cost Schedule and Quality Raised to the Third Power.

CSQ3® Fundamentals - are basic CSQ3® concepts and methodologies that are applicable to all work efforts.

CSQ3® Metrics - is an organizational performance scoring system. The maximum organizational score is 10,000 points. Six thousand of the ten thousand points are dedicated to the delivery of organizational value. The remaining four thousand points are dedicated to the development of a self-correcting organization. "Organizational Excellence" is achieved, when an organization scores 9,000 points or more.

CSQ3® Optimum - is a multilevel organizational work flow system. Key organizational work efforts are contained in each level. The three levels are Strategic, Major Commercial, and Project. The system is applicable to any organization. The system allows organizations to "Perform the Right Work, at the Right Time, with the Right People."

CSQ3® Quality - is the "Delivery of Actual Value" and the "Making of Sound Decisions."

Decision Point – is located in between work effort phases, where the decision is made to either stop, "Kill" the work effort or "Approve" the work effort to the next phase.

Decision Table – is a table containing the controllable and risk mitigation decisions and decision options considered by a work effort team. Decision options are chosen based on the risk tolerance of the work effort.

Detail Phase – is the "Meat on the Bones" division of any work effort. Cost, Schedule, and Value estimates are +/- 15%.

Execution Plus® - is a work effort documentation methodology that simplifies and standardizes the reporting requirements of work effort teams.

Functional Group – Personnel in a department that have specialized areas of expertise.

Functional Decisions – work effort decisions made by team members with specialized areas of expertise.

Fundamental Appraisal – Cost, Schedule, and Decision Quality review of a work effort.

Governance – is an organization's internal procedures to manage and insure the integrity of the CSQ3® Optimum and CSQ3® Metrics systems.

Implement Phase – is the "Make It Happen" division of any work effort.

Key Organizational Work Effort - is a work effort that requires multi-department input or is a department work effort designated by management to be included in the CSQ3® Optimum workflow system. All key organizational work efforts are to be included in the CSQ3® Optimum workflow system.

Major Commercial Level - is the accumulation of all major work efforts that have a significant (economic, political, or sociological) contractual impact on an organization.

Management Decision Point – is located in between work effort phases and is a formal review with a work effort team where management either stops "Kills" the work effort or "Approves" the work effort to the next phase.

Operate Phase – is the "Manage the Results" division of any work effort.

Organizational Excellence – A CSQ3® Metrics score of 9,000 points or more in the 10,000 point organizational performance scoring system.

Phase – identifiable division of work activity in a work effort.

Risk Mitigation Decisions – work effort decisions made by team members to minimize the negative effects of an uncontrollable event.

ROI – is Return on Investment. ROI equals (Revenues minus Investment) divided by Investment. Include intangibles or goodwill in the revenue term, as appropriate.

Inclusion of intangibles or goodwill should be consistent among all key organizational work efforts.

Project Level - is the accumulation of all work efforts that result in the building, construction, or development of tangible end products.

Schedule Estimate – is the estimated time for a work effort to reach the Operate Phase. Schedule estimates are provided at the end on the Concept, Structure, and Detail Phases with accuracies of +/- 40%, +/- 25%, and +/- 15%, respectively.

Strategic Level – is the accumulation of all work efforts that establish organizational direction.

Structure Phase – is the "Framework" division of any work effort. Cost, Schedule, and Value estimates are +/- 25%

The Business Roundtable - (www.businessroundtable.org) is an association of chief executive officers of leading U.S. companies

Ultimate Appraisal – is an organizational review of a work effort in the Operate Phase with the intent of establishing the Actual Delivered Value of the work effort.

Value Estimate – is the estimated value of a work effort. Report value in monetary terms, such as Return on Investment (ROI). Value estimates are provided at the end on the Concept, Structure, and Detail Phases with accuracies of +/- 40%, +/- 25%, and +/- 15%, respectively. Include Operating Phase costs and revenues. Include goodwill or intangibles, as appropriate.

Work Effort – has a definable objective; a start and an end point; numerous tasks or activities; and measurable results or goals.

LaVergne, TN USA
14 September 2010
196985LV00003B/3/P